Our Search with SOCRATES *for* MORAL TRUTH

GARY MICHAEL ATKINSON

Our Search with SOCRATES *for* MORAL TRUTH

THE CATHOLIC UNIVERSITY OF AMERICA PRESS
Washington, D.C.

The paper used in this publication meets the minimum
requirements of American National Standards for Information
Science—Permanence of Paper for Printed Library Materials,
ANSI Z39.48-1984.
∞

Library of Congress Cataloging-in-Publication Data
Atkinson, Gary Michael.
Our search with Socrates for moral truth /
Gary Michael Atkinson.
pages cm
Includes bibliographical references and index.
ISBN 978-0-8132-2785-6 (pbk.: alk. paper)
1. Ethics. 2. Plato. Dialogues. 3. Socrates. I. Title.
B398.E8A78 2015
170—dc23 2015016659

CONTENTS

APOLOGY *for* THIS BOOK

Apology (n.)—"Justification, explanation, or excuse, of an incident or course of action."

This book has been a long time in development, and its full significance has become clear to me only gradually: *no human life expresses the full human potential unless it contains (to some significant degree) the search for moral truth and the acquisition of moral knowledge*. An immediate corollary: any life totally lacking in that search and acquisition is to some degree defective, lacking in what ought to be there. These are by no means new claims, as we shall see, but they remain as radical as on the day they were first made. They are radical because they stand in sharp contradiction to four widely shared beliefs: (1) there is no such thing as moral truth; therefore, (2) there is no such thing as moral knowledge; therefore, (3) the search for moral truth and knowledge is necessarily a fruitless effort and waste of time; and furthermore, (4) the claim that any typical human life is defective is unsupported, foolish, or bigoted. This book is first of all a challenge to these widely shared beliefs. Its aim is to show what moral truth looks like and display the means by which moral knowledge is acquired. I begin this apology with a brief history of my professional adventures (and misadventures) in the college classroom in

All dictionary definitions in this book are drawn from the *Compact Edition of the Oxford English Dictionary* (Oxford: Oxford University Press, 1971).

order to explain how the idea for this book arose, and then suggest the strategy by which the existence of moral truth and knowledge will be defended.

A Brief History of My Moral Musings

I spend the bulk of my days trying to be a good college teacher. Most of my "work" goes into teaching an introductory course in ethics. I love teaching the course because I think it is very important, but I find each semester that a number of my students could not care less about taking the course—not all, but a much larger number than I would like. And it is not just me; my colleagues, some excellent and popular teachers among them, will tell you pretty much the same story—a surprising number of the students at my college just do not care much about the topics of the course itself. As one might imagine, I have devoted a considerable amount of time to mulling this over and stewing about it.

You might suppose that the fault lies somewhere with the students themselves, but that is not it. They are (generally) bright and well-motivated kids, and I really like them and enjoy interacting with them, though I admit they do laugh when I tell them that. And furthermore, the students at my college are hard-working—perhaps a bit too hard-working at their partying, but they will do what you ask them. You tell them to write three papers, and they will write three papers. Tell them to add footnotes, and they will.

When I think of ethics, I think of seeking to discover the very best life possible. I do not mean the questions of what to major in or what career path to choose or whom to marry—I mean the discovery of the "Big Picture" into which all the smaller pieces fit. What does the best life I can possibly live look like? In light of this, should I major in history or accounting, go into high school teaching or banking, marry sooner or later, marry this person or that?

Apology for This Book

Everyone, whether he recognizes it or not, has the rudiments of a Big Picture knocking around in his head somewhere. Certainly my students do. I say this because they have chosen to enter college and to enter my college and have hit upon a major or at least are thinking hard about one. And they could not have done any of these things unless they had a Big Picture lurking in the background somewhere in light of which they assess the competing merits and drawbacks of attending this college or that, adopting this major or that.

There are then two different kinds of questions. The single "Really Big Question"—what does the very best life I can possibly live look like, what are the rough contours of the Big Picture? And the many smaller, important but smaller, questions which engage us: given that the Big Picture looks like such-and-such, attending which college, taking which major, marrying which person will best contribute to living my life in accordance with my Big Picture?

We are not born with answers to the Really Big Question. The answer grows and develops mostly without our paying attention to what is happening. Some people have determinate outlines of their Big Picture from an astonishingly early age; most of us come upon it gradually. And we also know from our own experience or that of others that people's ideas about the Big Picture can undergo radical change. We often speak of these changes as "conversions," a real turning of the whole self, as it were, away from one way of life toward a radically different one. Perhaps more common is the experience of a Big Picture's becoming more filled out and detailed. There are things we miss at first glance, but after thinking about them a bit, experiencing them in a new light, we make a modification in the Big Picture without giving it up entirely. The relative importance of various features in our Big Picture can undergo shifts. Things we once valued highly become less valued or cease to be valued at all. Other things increase in importance as the years go by.

We may come to regret some of our past choices; we wish we could do them over again.

Let me explain with an example. Suppose my Big Picture of the very best life I can possibly lead is that of a life possessing lots and lots of money and lots and lots of toys to play with. (This cannot be the whole story, of course, but we want to keep things simple.) Given my goal, I have a basis from which to answer a variety of questions—whether to attend college at all and if so what college to attend, what major to select, what career to adopt, where to work, what firm to join, etc. Once I have an answer to the Really Big Question, a path to providing answers to these many smaller questions is opened up to me. I can decide which of two firms to join by determining their relative long-term prospects for salaries, bonuses, promotions, etc.

Obviously, the possession of an answer to the Really Big Question does not solve all of my problems. First, because figuring out which of the two firms really offers the best long-term prospects for income can be a real challenge. And second, because few of our decisions involve just one factor. Perhaps one firm has the best prospects, but I hate the city I would have to move to or the climate. Life is not a bed of roses. Even if I possess a clear Big Picture for myself, I am certain to face a lot of difficulties, encounter a lot of disappointments, but at least I will know where I am trying to go and I will know when I get there, if I ever do.

But imagine that at some point in my life I do get there and discover that it is really not where I wanted to go at all, that somewhere I had taken a false turn, which turns out to have been a terrible mistake because it is irreversible. Here I have spent most of my life pursuing a Big Picture that I once sort of grew into without much thought. I may now not even be able to explain to myself just how I came to believe that possessing all this stuff would be so great. But there it is, and my life has a big hole in it which cannot be filled. I missed the answer to the Really Big Question, and it will not be of much consolation to me to be reminded that my answers to the many smaller questions were stunningly good. So it is important to think hard about it, and to try to answer the Really Big Question as best we can. It is the most fundamental practical question there is, and an answer to it always comes in the form of a Big Picture. If we do not get it right, do not come up with an adequate Big Picture, then getting right all the smaller questions ultimately will not mean much of anything to us at all.

Perhaps the reader can now begin to understand the way I see the puzzle. On the one hand, my introductory ethics course is an inquiry into answering the Really Big Question and developing an adequate Big Picture for each of the students. It is a question that can be answered only by the students themselves. I provide a range of possible answers for students to reflect upon, and though I do not try to conceal my own preferences, I also do not try to push any answer, because doing so would be futile and counterproductive. I believe that the students by and large understand my hands-off approach. I want them to recognize first of all that they do in fact possess a Big Picture and have been using it throughout their post-childhood lives to guide their decisions. I also want them to understand the general contours of their Big Picture and to see how the considerations developed throughout the course bear upon it. Finally, I want the students to reassess and rethink their Big Picture, whether to throw it out completely (a most unlikely scenario) and start over, or to make some relatively minor adjustments, or to find themselves confirmed in their prior commitments.

On the other hand, a number of my students view my course quite differently, seeing it all as a royal waste of their time and money. A few will begin the course thinking it a waste and over the semester come to share my view of its worth. They tell me so. But others find it of no value from start to finish, and they tell me that, too. Although for different students I am sure there are a host of different explanations, there is one explanation I have hit upon which provides the theme of this book. One reason many students do not find the course to be of any value is that they do not believe in the possibility of the discovery of moral truth.

You cannot discover what you already see and hold in your hand. I suspect many of my students believe they already know what their Big Picture is, and that is good enough for them. They know what their general goals are, and the idea of their possibly being mistaken about those goals is an idea which seems never to have seriously bothered them. Their culture is not very big on the topic of wasted lives. Achieving your own vision of success, now that is big; avoiding the making of a huge mistake about your vision is not so big. What is your passion? If it works for you, go for it. Just do it. But how will you know if it works for you? And when will you know it? And if you know it today, will you know the same thing in ten or twenty years? Our culture is not particularly reflective about these matters, and I suggest that the principal reason for this is that our culture and the students who have been formed by our culture assume that there really is not very much to reflect upon, there really is not much to discover, because there really is not any *truth* about the Big Picture to be discovered. We all have our own Big Picture, and if your Big Picture differs radically from mine, who is to say who is right?

That question is generally taken to be the showstopper, playing the ace of trumps. Who is to say who is right? Answer: nobody. Why? Answer: because there is not any truth about the Big Picture in accordance with which someone could be correct and someone else mistaken. So, let each person do his own thing, pursue his life in accordance with *his* Big Picture, as long as he does not interfere with anyone else's pursuing a different way of life in accordance with a different Big Picture. "Live and let live" is the motto we all can and should stand by.

Question: what is the reason for thinking that "there is not any truth about the Big Picture in accordance with which someone could be correct and someone else mistaken"? We are coming here, I think, close to the heart of the matter. Answer: because if there were some truth about the Big Picture, there would be some sort of general agreement about it; but there obviously is not anything close to general agreement, so there cannot be any truth about the Big Picture.

Now is hauled out and upended a cornucopia of irresolvable and heated disagreements. Abortion, euthanasia, research using fetal stem cells, human cloning, genetic engineering and testing, selective abortion for undesired traits, drug use, premarital sex, polygamy, contraception, sex-change operations, gay marriage, gay adoption, animal rights, responsibilities to the environment, capital punishment, government surveillance of citizens, assassination, torture, preemptive military strikes, responsibilities to the poor, affirmative action, workers' rights, etc. And that is just within western culture. If we compare non-western cultures we can find disagreement regarding forced abortion, abortion for sex-selection, slavery, forced marriage, rights of minority religions and unbelievers, rights of nations to exist and be self-determined, genocide, targeted attacks on civilians, etc.

The argument is simple and straightforward. If (1) there were truth about the best way of conducting our lives, we would expect that (2) there would be common agreement about such matters; but we find nothing approaching such common agreement; therefore, there is no such truth about these matters. The argument pattern (called *modus tollens*): if (1) then (2), but not (2), and therefore not (1). If I were dreaming, then the pain caused by holding onto this red-hot poker would not be so intense, but the pain is intense, and therefore I am not dreaming.

Well, at least that is my solution to the puzzle. Pick just about any topic of moral discussion, and you will find at least two and often many opposed positions on the subject. But if there were a genuine truth about the topic, you would expect it to have been discovered by someone sooner or later and shown to others and the question would at some point have become settled. We would not think this about *every* such topic, but we would certainly expect to find this to be true of *some*, at least *one*, would we not? And do we find *any* resolved issue? Answer: no! And why? Answer: because there is no truth to be discovered. It is just a matter of what each person or culture believes, without any culture having evidence to support the truth of that belief.

I suspect that is roughly what at least some of my students believe. They believe just what their culture believes, and that is why they think my course will be of no worth to them. There is not any truth about the Big Picture, so there is not any way in which their Big Picture could be mistaken. They know that other people do not share their Big Picture, but that is okay. The lack of common agreement does not bother them at all because it does not show that they are mistaken. On the contrary, it shows they *cannot* be mistaken, and that is why my ethics course is for some of them, at least, a waste of time and money.

Let us call this the argument from unresolved widespread disagreement. It serves to distinguish respected fields of inquiry—the natural sciences, for instance—from suspect ones, such as philosophy generally and ethics in particular. We do not see universal agreement in the natural sciences, of course. New scientific questions are constantly arising; some are resolved quickly, some can hang around for a long time. But we do see genuine progress because there is a truth about the natural world to be discovered, hard as it may sometimes be to discover it. In sharp contrast, what do we find with the ethical "sciences"? Answer: no progress at all. Just the same old questions getting resurfaced and recycled and new questions arising to be added to the same old mix. And that is because there is no truth about the ethical world to be discovered as there is about the natural world. The ethical world is a funhouse of mirrors, and you can look into a mirror and see one shape and then shift your vision a bit and see in the same mirror a totally different shape.

The argument from unresolved widespread disagreement accounts, I suspect, for much of my students' disinclination to take the ethics course and for much of what passes for moral thought in their culture. Imposing one's values on others is a very bad thing indeed because it comes down to *your* forcing *me* to do things I do not want to do simply because you want me to do them. And that is a very bad thing indeed, unless it is a matter of *my* forcing *you* to do things you do not want to do simply because I want you to do them, and that is okay and proper because that is different. Critical self-awareness and rational consistency are not among the long suits of my students' culture.

The Strategy of This Book

The argument from unresolved widespread disagreement is mistaken, and the aim of this book is to show why. That there exists unresolved widespread disagreement no one in his right mind would deny. The conclusion that is supposed to follow from its existence is where the mistake enters. It is easy to point out the place where the mistake occurs, but it will take this entire book to prove it.

When we think of a disagreement, we think of two or more

people who hold different opinions on some topic. Let us call them "researchers." I think it will immediately be clear to everyone that we can distinguish two kinds of researchers, "qualified" versus "unqualified." By a qualified researcher I mean a person who possesses whatever traits are necessary or helpful for discovering the truth about the topic, assuming there is indeed a truth to be discovered. An unqualified researcher, in contrast, lacks one or more of those traits.

Three points. First, the qualified/unqualified distinction is a matter of degree. There may be few or no perfectly qualified researchers on a given topic. It may be that all researchers possess some qualifications; none of them is completely unqualified. Second, it can happen that a more qualified researcher is mistaken on a particular point, while the less qualified researcher is correct. We expect qualified researchers to be more often correct than unqualified ones, but that is true only generally and over the long run. In any particular case we may hold a presumption in favor of the more qualified researcher's views, but that is only a presumption which may not be correct about the topic at hand. Finally, some uncertainty may arise about who is or is not a qualified researcher, either because of disagreement regarding the features one needs to be qualified or because of disagreement regarding whether a given researcher possesses them.

So what is *the* point? The point of drawing the distinction between qualified and unqualified researchers is that doing so serves to highlight what does and does not follow from the existence of unresolved widespread disagreement in a given area of inquiry. Take first the field of the natural sciences. Because we already believe there are genuine truths out there about the world of nature which the natural sciences are striving with some success to reach, we are not inclined to pay much attention to disagreement over a particular issue, even when the disagreement is longstanding and the researchers who disagree are all very well qualified. In the natural sciences we do not find unresolved widespread disagreement, so the existence of particular disagreements, even when longstanding, does not lead us to believe that there simply is no truth to be had about the matter. The qualified researchers have not been able to figure it all out just yet. But in the field of the ethical "sciences" a different story can be told. The existence of particular disagreements is taken to possess different significance here because there is no background of general widespread agreement against which to assess particular disagreements. On the contrary, particular disagreements are simply more instances of what we have already noted regarding the ethical "sciences," that there is no general agreement at all, no general agreement about anything. And that is supposed to show, as we have noted, that there is not any truth about the ethical "sciences" to be had, that it is all a matter of feelings and emotions and desires and preferences.

Yes, but this unresolved widespread disagreement that we find among researchers in the ethical "sciences," is this a disagreement between researchers who are qualified or unqualified? This is a vital question to raise and to answer, because *the existence of unresolved disagreement among unqualified researchers, as such, has no significance whatsoever*. Remember, an unqualified researcher is one who lacks traits necessary or helpful for discovering the truth about a particular topic, assuming there exists a truth to be discovered. Let us take two totally unqualified researchers: they possess none of the traits necessary or helpful for discovering the truth about the topic under investigation. And they disagree. Question: so what? Answer: absolutely nothing at all. So you and I put on blindfolds, and then colored pieces of paper are presented to us and we are asked to name their color, and we do not agree and cannot come to an agreement about their color. And this shows ... nothing. If we are dealing with researchers whom we recognize to be unqualified, their agreement as such shows nothing about whether there is a truth regarding the matter or what that truth is, and their disagreement, even if unresolved and widespread, does nothing to establish that there is no truth.

Well, this example with you and me in blindfolds—is it an image of the ethical "sciences" or is it not? Are the vast majority of ethical researchers qualified or are they not? Suppose there was (1) unresolved widespread disagreement among the unqualified researchers, (2) unresolved widespread disagreement between the unqualified researchers and the qualified researchers, and (3) no unresolved widespread disagreement among the qualified researchers themselves. I am not saying that this is so; I am saying, suppose it were so. What then?

Hold on there, one might interject. Who is to say who is a qualified researcher and who is not? Well, first, is there any unresolved widespread disagreement about the traits of qualified researchers in ethics? I am unaware that the question has ever been raised, at least in this form; or if it has, I am unaware that it has received widespread attention. Not having received widespread attention, widespread disagreement regarding it can hardly exist. Second, it may be that the traits of a qualified researcher can be recognized by someone who himself is not a qualified researcher. In other words, the answer to the question of who is a qualified researcher in ethics may be available without prejudice, without begging any questions at all.

In fact, the inquiry of this book is a defense of the claim that the question of who is a qualified researcher in ethics is in principle no different from analogous questions regarding any other field of inquiry. You need not yourself be a qualified researcher in order to recognize what the traits of a qualified researcher are. You do not yourself need to possess a particular trait in order to recognize that it would be necessary or at least of great help in discovering truth, if indeed there were any truth to be discovered. This inquiry proceeds, then, without assuming there is any such thing as ethical truth at all. *Nothing* in any way controversial is assumed. We start from what we know. As every new trait is uncovered, there is one and only one question to be addressed: is there clear and compelling reason to believe that an ideally qualified researcher in the field of ethics must possess the trait under consideration? (If you would like a peek at where we are going to wind up, the final list of traits can be found in the general conclusion.)

An ideally qualified researcher in the field of ethics is a person who is best able to answer the Really Big Question—what is the best kind of life I can make for myself, the best life I can possibly lead? Such a person who is best able to discover the truth about the Big Picture, assuming there might indeed exist a truth to be discovered. But, to forestall a possible misunderstanding, I should point out that the assumption that there may exist a truth about the Big Picture does not mean that there is only one true Big Picture. There could be lots of different kinds of lives which are the best kinds of lives for different kinds of people. The true Big Picture for you may depend considerably on personal circumstances, predilections, and choice; it may look considerably different from my true Big Picture. Furthermore, for a single individual there may be several equally true Big Pictures differing from one another in considerable degree. The suggestions of a true answer to the Really Big Question and a true Big Picture are not intended to suggest rigid conformity or constraint. Let a thousand flowers bloom! The only point is that there may be a truth, and wherever there is a truth there is also the possibility of mistake and error.

How shall we begin? Since we are facing a task in ethical philosophy, and since (as Alfred North Whitehead observed) Western philosophy is nothing other than "a series of footnotes to Plato" (427–347 B.C.), we may profitably turn to the master himself and to his teacher and hero Socrates (470–399 B.C.) for help. Plato's dialogues present Socrates as a person who at times astonishes us with the intensity of his search for truth. In the course of the dialogues Socrates encounters a host of strongly delineated figures who may or may not share perfectly in that search. By attending closely to Socrates and those with whom he speaks, we will find ourselves encountering the traits we are looking for and their polar opposites. Let us see what we can glean from watching Socrates go about his search for ethical truth.

Translations from the Greek sources are mine, and I have tried to preserve the syntax of the Greek sentences as best I could. Parenthetical citations use the standard system for referring to passages in the Platonic corpus, the so-called Stephanus number.[1] Citations to the works of Aristotle (384–322 B.C.), Plato's pupil, employ the standard Bekker number.

1. All citations of Platonic dialogues are to *Platonis Opera* (5 vols.), eds. John Burnet et al. (Oxford: Oxford University Press, 1901–2011).

PART 1

THE TRUTH, *the* WHOLE TRUTH, *and* NOTHING *but* *the* TRUTH

1

LACHES, GORGIAS, *and the* EXPERT

Expert (n.) "Trained by experience or practice, skilled, skillful."

Experience (n.) "The actual observation of facts or events, considered as a source of knowledge."

Definition (n.) "A precise statement of the essential nature of a thing."

Let us begin with the *Laches*. As is true for most of Plato's dialogues, this one's title is taken from the name of a principal figure in the dialogue, the famous general Laches. In the dialogue appear another famous general, Nicias, and two men besides Socrates, Lysimachus and Melesias, each of whom has a son and wishes to provide the best education to help the young man become as excellent as possible. Someone had suggested to the fathers that their sons be taught how to fight in armor, and so the fathers are interested to hear what the two distinguished generals think about the matter. The generals both express a readiness to assist the fathers in their project, but Laches urges them to include Socrates here in their inquiry, for he is a man who "is always spending his time here where there is investigation into the very things you are searching for, the study and training appropriate for the youth" (180c). Acting upon

Laches's advice, Lysimachus puts the fathers' question to Socrates, who expresses a readiness to help as best he can, but rather than offer his own answer, he defers to the generals who are older and have more experience in these subjects. Unfortunately, the generals hold different opinions on the question. Nicias believes that the knowledge of how to fight in armor is helpful to the young in all sorts of ways; but Laches disagrees with Nicias, claiming he had never encountered any practitioner of the art of fighting in armor who had ever become famous in war, and he asks Socrates for his opinion. Lysimachus concurs with Laches's request, pointing out that given the generals' disagreement, Socrates is needed to break the tie. Socrates's response is characteristic of him and highly instructive (184d–185a):

S: Really, Lysimachus; whatever the majority of us recommends, are you going to rely on *them*?

L: What else should I do, Socrates?

S: And you, Melesias, would you do the same? If you had to make a decision regarding the gymnastic training of your son, how he should exercise, would you obey the majority of us, or the one who had been taught by and practiced under a skillful trainer?

M: Following that one, Socrates, would surely be reasonable.

S: So you would obey him rather than the four of us?

M: Very likely.

S: Because I think a person wanting to make a good decision must rely on knowledge and not on the majority?

M: Of course.

S: So, we must first of all ask this very thing, whether any of us is an expert in what we are deliberating about, or not? If there is, then to obey him, even though he's only one, and forget the others. If there's not, then to search out someone else.

This focus on the expert and the possession of expertise is one that no reader of the dialogues can miss. It seems to be almost an obsession with Socrates. Witness his response to the orator Gorgias in the dialogue of the same name. Gorgias is a sophist, a travelling teacher, who has come to Athens to instruct the young men in the "most admirable" of all crafts, the art or skill of oratory (or rhetoric). As a travelling teacher, Gorgias must find students willing to pay him for imparting to them his skill in oratory. Socrates expresses a desire to assist Gorgias in finding such students by encouraging him to explain precisely what his skill of oratory is and what it does that makes it so admirable and thus valuable and thus well worth the money of the young men (or their fathers). In short, Gorgias needs to provide Socrates and his prospective students with a definition of what oratory is, an account of its nature.

Gorgias attempts to oblige Socrates, and after a considerable number of false steps offers the following as a definition of what oratory (as he conceives and teaches it) is and does: "The ability to persuade with speeches judges and jurors in a law court, councilors in council-chamber, assemblymen in a public assembly, and in any other political gathering" (452e). This power, this ability to persuade in any and all political contexts, is for Gorgias the supreme power, the effect of the "most admirable" of crafts, for by this power the craft of oratory subordinates to itself all other skills and crafts. As he immediately adds: "With this power you will have the physician as your slave, the trainer as your slave, and the money-maker will be seen to be making money for someone else and not for himself, for *you* the powerful one who can speak and persuade multitudes" (452e). And how is this? Because in the political gathering the pupil who has become the expert orator through Gorgias's ministrations will be able to persuade the citizens—assemblymen, judges, councilors, jurors—about the course of action to be adopted by the political body before which the orator speaks. By mastering the craft of oratory, you will be able to promote your friends to high offices and have your enemies fined, imprisoned, or exiled. Because of your skill in oratory, no one will be able to hold his ground against you.

Yes, but this unchallenged ability to persuade, Socrates asks, what *kind* of persuasion does it produce in the mind of its hearers (454cd)?

S: Is there something you call "having learned"?

G: Yes.

S: And also "having believed"?

G: Yes.

S: And do "having learned" and "having believed" seem to you to be the same or different, knowledge and belief the same or different?

G: I think they are different, Socrates.

S: And you think correctly, as you can see from this: if someone were to ask you "Gorgias, is there such a thing as a false belief as well as a true belief?" you would answer "yes," or so I think.

G: Yes.

S: But, is there false knowledge as well as true?

G: Certainly not.

S: So it is clear then that these things, knowledge and belief, are not the same.

Socrates's point is first a linguistic one, true of Greek and true of the English language too, for that matter. It is thoroughly good English or Greek to say that someone has a false belief, but not to say that so-and-so's knowledge is false. If we call it knowledge, we cannot say it is false; if we say it is false, we cannot call it knowledge. Gorgias immediately understands Socrates's point about correct Greek usage.

But now the question: this persuasion which the skilled orator is capable of effecting in the minds of his hearers, is it belief-persuasion or is it knowledge-persuasion? The hearers now have a belief, but is that belief also knowledge (which cannot be false) or is it mere belief (which might be true but which also might be false)? Gorgias immediately understands the point of Socrates's question and answers unhesitatingly—the belief which the hearer possesses is indeed mere belief, it is not knowledge. Socrates agrees with Gorgias's answer, adding in support that "he could not teach such a crowd such important matters in a short time" (455a). By "teach" Socrates means "impart knowledge," and by "short time" he means the average length of a political speech.

So, if we are to believe Gorgias, the skill of oratory is the most admirable of all skills because it provides its possessor with the power of all powers, the power to subdue to itself all other arts and skills. *And yet* it produces no knowledge at all but only mere belief. But how can Gorgias's remarks both be true, Socrates asks (455bc):

> When there is a meeting in the city concerning the selection of physicians or shipbuilders or any other kind of craftsman, the orator will not advise then, will he? It is clear that in each choice it is the one ablest in the craft who must be selected. Or when, in the building of walls or in the construction of harbors or docks, it is the master craftsmen. Or when an assembly is held for the selection of generals or the preparations necessary against an enemy or the seizure of territory, then the military leaders will advise, the rhetoricians not.

Imagine I were to inform you that although I am not a real doctor, I am nonetheless highly adept at persuading people about the state of their health. So if you ever have any question of a personal medical nature, rather than going through the rigmarole of setting up an appointment at a real doctor's office and then making the round trip to get checked out, you could instead just catch me at some free moment and I will be happy to persuade you regarding your condition and what if anything needs to be done about it. Am I correct in thinking you might hesitate to take me up on my generous offer? I bet you have the same attitude toward the matter as Socrates had in the passage from the *Laches* already quoted: "If you had to make a decision regarding the gymnastic training of your son, how he should exercise, would you obey the majority of us, or the one who had been taught by and practiced under a skillful trainer?" (184e).

2

MENO, KNOWLEDGE, *and* TRUTH

Knowledge (n.) "Intellectual acquaintance with, or perception of, fact or truth; clear and certain mental apprehension."

Truth (n.) "Conformity with fact; agreement with reality; accuracy, correctness, verity (of statement or thought)."

The *Meno* opens abruptly with a peremptory question from a young man (Meno) who Socrates suspects knows himself to be the very handsome young man he in fact is: "Can you tell me, Socrates, whether virtue is teachable; or if not teachable, whether it is acquired by practice, or if neither by practice nor teaching, whether it comes to men by nature or in some other way?" (70a). Socrates responds in characteristic fashion to Meno's opening question by saying that he is unable to answer and does not even know what virtue itself is.[1] Meno finds Socrates's second disclaimer nearly unbelievable. Really, Socrates does not even know what virtue is? Yes, and Socrates makes the even more astounding claim that he has

1. As in the *Gorgias* (with "oratory"), Socrates will be in the hunt for the definition of a key term.

never met anyone who did know. Does Meno know what virtue is? Yes, certainly. Well then, speak it out, do not leave us in suspense! "It will not be at all difficult to tell you, Socrates" (71e).

Well, you might not be too surprised to be told there turns out to be considerable difficulty. In fact, as a result of Socrates's acute questions, Meno is finally brought to confess (80ab):

> Now really, I find my mind and my mouth are numb, and I do not have anything I can answer you. And yet many times have I delivered lengthy speeches on the topic of virtue before large audiences, and very good ones too, at least so it seemed to me. But now, I can say nothing about what virtue is. I think you would be well advised not to sail away from here and live elsewhere, because if you did this sort of thing as a foreigner in another city, you might be driven away for being a wizard.[2]

Since neither Socrates nor Meno, as it turns out, knows what virtue is, it is going to be extremely difficult to answer Meno's opening question. If you do not know what P is, how are you supposed to discover how P is acquired? But Socrates suggests a strategy which may offer some hope of finding their way out of this impasse. His suggestion is to consider the possibility that virtue is a form of knowledge; if it were, one would think that virtue could be taught. Those who possess the knowledge that is virtue would, one thinks, be able to convey their knowledge to their pupils; there would be teachers of this knowledge and learners of it.

2. One might puzzle over Meno's imagining Socrates's "sailing away and living elsewhere," since Socrates was famous for his devotion and attachment to the city of his birth. The dialogue *Crito*, set in prison after Socrates's trial but before his execution, presents his friend Crito as strenuously urging Socrates to do just that. We will examine a bit of that dialogue in chapter 11. It is also clear that Plato intends the reader to pick up on the unconscious irony of Meno's remark. Socrates, as the history books and Plato tell us, was "driven away for being a wizard" neither by another city nor by Athens herself. He was in fact convicted and executed by the Athenian citizens for precisely the same kind of pointed questioning ("wizardry") he displays in his dealing with Meno. In our dialogue a rather unpleasant character is soon to join Meno and Socrates, a friend of Meno named Anytus. This figure will turn out to be one of Socrates's accusers at his trial. The second half of the *Meno* is heavy with foreboding.

But if Socrates has no idea what virtue is, why does he offer the suggestion that virtue is a form of knowledge? Why select *that* as a possibility to consider over any one of a host of others? Socrates's reason for focusing on the possibility of virtue as a kind of knowledge is arresting. It is because we know that *true* virtue has a feature that knowledge possesses. And what is that feature? Answer: the feature of being *always and necessarily beneficial* (87d–88a):

S: Do we maintain that virtue is anything other than something good, or does this assumption remain firm for us, that virtue is good?

M: Certainly.

S: Well, if what is good were something different from knowledge, then virtue [something good] might not be knowledge. But if there is nothing good which knowledge does not encompass, we would be right in suspecting that virtue is a kind of knowledge.

M: That would be so.

S: And it is because of virtue that we are good?

M: Yes.

S: And if good, then beneficial. All good things are beneficial. Yes?

M: Of course.

S: So virtue is something beneficial?

M: That necessarily follows from what we have agreed upon.

S: Now let us examine this, taking up one by one what sort of things benefit us: health, we say, and strength and handsome appearance and wealth, certainly—these things and things like them we call beneficial. Yes?

M: Yes.

S: Yet these very same things, we say, sometimes cause harm. Or would you disagree?

M: No, that is so.

And this difference among the beneficial things is accounted for by something of the utmost importance (88a–c):

S: Now look at this. When do we think any one of these benefits us, when does it harm? Is it not that when there is *right use* they benefit, when there is not right use they harm?

M: Certainly.

S: And we must also examine mental qualities. What do you say about temperance, justice, courage, being a quick learner, good memory, magnanimity, and all such?

M: Certainly.

S: So look at any of these qualities that seem to you not to be knowledge but something apart from knowledge. Is it not the case that sometimes they harm, sometimes they benefit? Courage, for instance, without good sense is a kind of presumption.[3] Is it not true that when someone is confident without intelligence he suffers harm, but with intelligence he is benefitted?

M: Yes.

S: The same for temperance and being a quick learner. United with intelligence, learning and training are beneficial things, without intelligence they are harmful things.

M: Very much so.

S: In summary, *everything undertaken or endured by the human spirit when guided by wisdom finds its completion in happiness, when guided by folly in its opposite.*

The wisdom or knowledge which is always beneficial is the wisdom or knowledge of "right use," the knowledge of how to use one's possessions, talents, and abilities in a way that is beneficial. Lacking that knowledge or wisdom, the possessor of any other trait *cannot* be sure of *always* using that talent or ability in a beneficial manner, and so the goodness and worth of *every* talent or possession, no matter what it might be, depends upon the possessor's *also* possessing the wisdom of "right use," the knowledge of how to use that talent well. Since virtue (at least according to Socrates) is something *always and necessarily beneficial*, virtue must be that wisdom, that knowledge of "right use." But if virtue is a form of knowledge and wisdom, then it should be teachable, and there should be teachers and pupils of virtue. Where to find them?

3. "Courage" then, like "temperance" in Socrates's following remark, may not always be the name of a *true* virtue if "virtue is something good" and "virtue is always and necessarily beneficial."

At this point a fortunate event occurs. Meno is not himself a citizen of Athens but has been visiting a friend, Anytus, who just now stumbles into the conversation. The man is a person of outstanding background and qualifications; surely we ought to include him. So, Anytus, since virtue appears to be a kind of knowledge, where are we to go to find its teachers and pupils? Should we not go to the sophists, teachers (like Gorgias) who travel from city to city and make their living by the teaching of virtue (91c–92c)?

A: By Heracles, Socrates, be silent! May no such madness ever seize anyone of my household or my friends, fellow citizen or foreigner, as to go to such people and be mutilated by them, for they clearly are the disgrace and corruption of whoever associates with them! ...

S: Has one of the sophists wronged you, Anytus, that you are so hard on them?

A: No, by Zeus, I have never met a single one of them, nor would I allow any one of my associates to do so, ever!

S: So you are *entirely without any experience* of these men?

A: Yes, and may I ever be so!

S: So how is it, my marvelous fellow, that you know whether there's anything good or anything bad in associating with them, a thing about which you are completely inexperienced?

A: Easily, for I know what those people are, whether or not I have experience of them.

S: Perhaps you are a diviner, Anytus, for I wonder, from the things you yourself say, how else you would know about them.

Well, if not the sophists, then who (92e–93b)?

A: But why is it necessary to mention the name of a particular individual? Any one of the Athenian gentlemen whom he chances to meet will make him better than the sophists would, if he is only willing to follow that one's advice.

S: And did these gentlemen become such on their own, learning from no one but none the less being able to teach others, able to teach what they themselves have not learned?

A: I think they learned it from those who came before them, those who were themselves gentlemen, or does it not seem to you that there are many good men in this city?

S: Anytus, there do seem to me to be good men here who involve themselves in politics, and no fewer in the past. But *this* has been the point of our discussion—have the good men also been teachers of their own virtue—not whether there are good men here or not, and not whether there have been good men in the past. From the start we have been asking: is virtue teachable?

Socrates goes on to consider some famous Athenian statesmen whom everyone would recognize to have been good and virtuous men. If they were virtuous and virtue is indeed a form of knowledge and virtue is therefore something teachable, then these famous statesmen would have been virtuous and therefore knowledgeable and presumably capable of teaching it, this knowledge of "right use." And if they were capable of teaching it, would they not in fact have taught it, at least to their own sons who would therefore have learned it and become virtuous and outstanding themselves? All this seems plausible, and yet when Socrates runs through his list of famous statesmen—he mentions four of them—and examines the lives of their sons, he finds that none of the latter ultimately amounted to much of anything. How can this be? That the statesmen were virtuous no one disputes. They would certainly have wanted to make their sons equally virtuous had they been able to do so, and they did in fact take pains with their sons' education. How can virtue then be a form of knowledge and therefore teachable? The answer is that it cannot. Where then did we go wrong?

Anytus, as it turns out, has ceased to pay attention to the logic of Socrates's argument or to be seized by the perplexity in which Socrates now finds himself. He is fixated on what he takes to be Socrates's slander of the famous statesmen for their failure to teach their sons virtue and make them virtuous and good (94e–95a).

A: You seem to me, Socrates, far too quick to speak evil of people. My advice to you, if you will but listen to me, is to take care. It is likely that in another city it is far easier to harm someone than to do him good, and that is very much the case here, as I think you yourself well know.[4]

S: Meno, Anytus seems to me to be angry, and I am not at all surprised. He thinks first of all I am slandering those politicians, and then he believes himself to be one of them. If he really knew what it was to speak evil of someone, he would get over his anger, but as it is he is ignorant.

Anytus says not another word in the dialogue, but Plato makes clear that Anytus remains none the less, listening, but perhaps understanding not a whit.

And the puzzle remains, too: if virtue seems to be a particular kind of knowledge because both of them are something always and everywhere beneficial, why did the virtuous Athenian statesmen not teach their knowledge/virtue to their sons, thus making them virtuous and outstanding themselves? Socrates himself suggests what he believes to be an answer to his puzzle (97a–c):

S: If someone knows the road to Larissa, or wherever else he might wish to go and bring others along, he would guide correctly and well, would he not?

M: Certainly.

S: But if a man believes correctly which is the road, never himself having gone there and not knowing, does he not also guide correctly?

M: Certainly.

S: So, as long as he retains his correct opinion on the topic about which the other person knows, he will in no way be a worse guide than the other who knows, believing the truth but not knowing it.

M: No worse at all.

S: So true opinion, as far as it pertains to correct action, is no worse a guide than knowledge. And this very thing is what we just now left out in

4. Any reader at all familiar with the facts of Socrates's impending (unjust?) trial and execution will detect the irony of Anytus's remark.

our investigation of what virtue is, saying that knowledge alone guides us in right action. There is also true belief.

M: Very likely.

S: So true belief is no less beneficial than knowledge.

Socrates thinks that this similarity between knowledge and true belief resolves the apparent paradox. On the one hand, we thought that virtue must be knowledge because virtue is always beneficial and the only thing which seemed to be always beneficial is knowledge of "right use." On the other hand, we inferred that the excellent statesmen of the past, whom we took to be virtuous, did *not* themselves possess knowledge because *had* they been knowledgeable they would have taught their sons this knowledge and the sons would have been virtuous as well, which we all acknowledge they were not.

But now our puzzle is resolved. It is not true that the only thing always beneficial is knowledge. We now see that true belief is as valuable as knowledge for purposes of acting rightly and advantageously. The great statesmen were virtuous, yes, and of great benefit to their cities. But we may not infer from this fact that they possessed knowledge; maybe they only possessed true belief. Possessing true belief, they were as valuable to their cities as they would have been had they possessed knowledge. But possessing only true belief and not knowledge, the virtuous statesmen did not teach their sons virtue and their sons did not become virtuous because the virtuous statesmen simply *could not* teach virtue, even though they had every reason for doing so. Though this solves the puzzle, it leaves us right back where we started with Meno's opening question: "Can you tell me, Socrates, whether virtue is teachable; or if not teachable, whether it is acquired by practice; or if neither by practice nor teaching, whether it comes to men by nature or in some other way?" (70a). All this talk and we have gained nothing—that's philosophy for you.

But it is not true that we have gained nothing. We have gained a great deal, but we need to step back a bit and reflect on what we have gained. We should pay close attention to Socrates's example of knowing the way to Larissa, for it is highly instructive. The example suggests that we can think of belief as something like a mental map. I am now looking at a map of Greece. I see that the part of the map marked Larissa lies in northeastern Greece along the Aegean Sea. I read that Larissa is part of the larger region of Thessaly. I estimate from the map that the region of Larissa is about a hundred miles north-northwest of Athens. From my investigation I now have a mental map of Greece generally and of Larissa in particular. If I were in Athens and wanted to travel to Larissa, I would have an idea about the direction I should take. I should aim roughly north and once I have hit the Aegean coast I should hold to it, expecting to reach Larissa after travelling about a hundred miles.

My goal is to reach Larissa. My action is one of travelling. My action is based on and governed by a map in my head. The mental map may be an image, but it also might just be a belief about Greece and Larissa. I will be likely to reach my goal if my action, my journey, is based on a belief which has "conformity with fact" of the geography of Greece, if it has "agreement with reality," if it has "accuracy, correctness, verity"—in short, if my belief is true. On the other hand, a journey to Larissa is unlikely to be successful if the belief/map upon which I act is not in conformity with the facts of Greek geography, if it does not agree with the reality which is the Greek mainland. True beliefs are desired and desirable because they contribute to successful action; false beliefs, on the other hand, are shunned because they greatly reduce the probability of successful action. True beliefs are accurate maps, false beliefs are inaccurate maps, and actions can be viewed as a kind of journey from where I presently am to where I want to be.

The language of "contribute to" and "reduce the probability of" is deliberate. Just because I have a true belief does not assure my action will be successful. And acting on a false belief does not assure that my action will fail. I can set out on the road to Larissa with an accurate map in my hand or head and be mugged by bandits. I can believe that Larissa is in the Peloponnese but get disoriented and think I am heading due west while in fact I am travelling north-northwest. Truth is no guarantee of successful action, nor does falsity preclude successful action, but certainly one's chances of success are greatly increased if our maps are accurate, if our beliefs are true.

What seems to matter, then, is simply that our belief-maps are true and accurate and correspond to the facts, to reality. It does not seem to matter, for purposes of successful action, whether our true beliefs merely happen to be true or whether they are grounded on some sort of expertise, grounded on experience, on "some clear and certain mental apprehension." To return to Socrates's example, you will reach Larissa just the same whether you follow the directions of a person familiar with the area or the directions of someone who just made them up on a lark and by sheer luck hit on the correct ones. But this insistence by Socrates on the sufficiency of true belief Meno finds troubling. In response to Socrates's assertion quoted above that "true opinion, as far as it pertains to correct action, is no worse a guide than knowledge," Meno objects (97cd):

> M: But in that respect, Socrates, the person with knowledge will always hit upon the right action, the person with right opinion sometimes yes, sometimes no.
>
> S: Really? The person preserving right opinion, will he not always hit upon the correct action as long as he believes correctly?
>
> M: Necessarily, or so it seems to me. But this being the case, I am now puzzled, Socrates, why knowledge is so much more prized than correct belief, and how there is a difference between them?

A very good question to ask Socrates. After all, was not *he* the one in the *Gorgias* who insisted that when the community is called upon to make some important decision, the expert with knowledge is the one *always* called upon? Was not *he* the one who questioned Gorgias's high regard for his craft of oratory after Gorgias admitted straight out that his craft produced only belief and not knowledge? Socrates recognizes the importance of the possession of true beliefs. The possession of the truth, a more or less accurate map of reality, is by far the best basis we can possibly have for successful action. But now, Socrates must explain the importance he places upon expertise and knowledge, since he himself admits that they are no more useful for successful action than is true belief without knowledge and expertise.

Socrates's response here contains a bright diamond, one of the many with which the dialogues are studded and which by themselves would be sufficient to establish Plato as a literary genius of the first rank. Socrates recalls to Meno's mind an image taken from the Greek myths. The reason for Meno's puzzlement regarding the superiority of knowledge over correct opinion, Socrates remarks, "is because you have not reflected upon the statues of Daedalus. Perhaps there are not any where you're from" (97d). If Meno had ever seen one of Daedalus's statues, he would immediately have understood the importance of knowledge over true belief.

You remember Daedalus. He was a sculptor whose works were so lifelike that when he had put the finishing touches on them they ... came alive! Now if you have never yourself seen one of Daedalus's statues, you may not immediately have grasped Socrates's point, but here it is: a statue sculpted by Daedalus would be a wonderful thing to possess, *provided* you had made sure that it would not be stolen *and* that it did not run away on its own, like one of your slaves. A statue of Daedalus, wonderful as it is, could not be of much value to you if you were unable to prevent its being stolen or its taking off on its own. Socrates's point (97e–98a):

> Why am I talking about this? True opinions, as long as they remain where they are, are lovely things and produce all sorts of good. *But* they do not like to remain where they are very long, and they run away from a person's mind, and so are not worth much *until* someone binds them down *with an account of the reason*.... But once they are tied down, then they become knowledge and are *fixed*. And this is why knowledge is more valuable than correct belief. Knowledge differs from correct belief by the presence of a fetter.

The statues of Daedalus, because they are so valuable, require fetters constructed of chains or ropes. True beliefs, again because of their worth, require a fetter as well. *This* "fetter" is "an account of the reason." The Greek here is *aitias logismō*, "with an account of the cause." What gives knowledge its "intellectual acquaintance with, perception of, fact or truth," its "clear and certain mental apprehension"? It is the possession of an account or explanation of why something is the case, an understanding which is the "intellectual acquaintance" with the fact or truth, an acquaintance which mere belief, even true belief, does not and cannot provide.

Have you ever had the experience of changing your mind about some issue, only to discover later that your first belief was the correct one and that you had made a mistake in changing it? And how did this happen? Socrates's answer: you had a correct belief, but it was not "tied down" by the "clear and certain mental apprehension" which is knowledge, and so was unstable and easily "lost." True belief would suffice for successful action if true belief were fixed and stable, were unlikely to be exchanged for false belief. But mere belief is as such always necessarily unstable, for it is not the "intellectual acquaintance" which only knowledge brings. As Socrates states: "I have been speaking not as one who knows but only using a likeness. But as for there being a difference between correct belief and knowledge, on that I do not at all believe I am merely guessing. If there were anything else I would say I know, and I would say there are few, I would set this as one of the things I know" (98b). This is why we seek knowledge and expertise from the experts. We desire *not only* (1) true belief itself, a reasonably accurate map of reality, the possession of which is something vital for successful action, *but also* (2) the stability of truth which only knowledge, and not mere true belief as such, can bring.

Have we written the final chapter on truth? Have we said everything that needs to be said? Well, as it turns out, no. Not everyone seems to care very much about finding out the truth, and this fact provides a subject for some serious reflection.

3

EUTHYPHRO and DESIRE

Desire (n.)—"That feeling or emotion which is directed to the attainment or possession of some object from which pleasure or satisfaction is expected; longing, craving."

Incurious (adj.)—"Not desirous of obtaining knowledge, information, or news; uninquisitive, uninquiring, indifferent; devoid of curiosity."

The *Euthyphro* is a good dialogue to study after the *Meno* because in one respect it picks up an undercurrent from the earlier dialogue. The unpleasant figure of Anytus who appears only midway through the *Meno* will turn out to be one of Socrates's accusers at his trial. We will get to that trial as presented in the dialogue *Apology* in the next chapter, but here the *Euthyphro* opens with Socrates on his way to court to defend himself from the twin charges of having introduced new gods into Athens and of having corrupted its young men. Euthyphro is also on his way to court, but in his case he will be serving as prosecutor. And who is the defendant? Someone, Euthyphro admits, whom people think he is a maniac for attacking—someone who is rather old, his father, in fact. His father? Yes. And the charge? Murder (4ab):

S: By Heracles! The majority would be ignorant of how to do such a thing in the right way, Euthyphro. I think that it is not the part of just anyone to do this in the right way but only for someone already far advanced in wisdom.

E: By Zeus, Socrates, far advanced.

S: The man killed by your father was a member of your family? Of course he was. For the death of anyone else you would never prosecute your father.

E: Laughable it is, Socrates, that you think it matters at all whether the dead man was a member of my family or someone else. The only thing to keep in mind is whether the killer killed with justice, or not.

If the killing was unjust, the killer must be prosecuted even if he shares your hearth, Socrates, and sits at your table, for the pollution remains if you do not cleanse yourself and him by bringing him to justice. Amazing! And what are the facts of the case? Well, one day a worker hired by Euthyphro's family got drunk and became angry with one of the house slaves and slit his throat. Euthyphro's father had the killer bound and thrown into a ditch; he then sent to Athens to seek direction from a seer about what should be done, but before the messenger returned the killer died from exposure. That is why Euthyphro's father and other relatives are angry with him for the prosecution. They say first that his father did not kill the man; second, that even if he did, the dead man was himself a murderer and not worthy of this consideration; and third, they say that it is impious for a son to prosecute his father for murder. "How poorly they understand, Socrates, how the divine stands with respect to the pious and the impious" (4e). Socrates is as flabbergasted as Euthyphro's father and family are angry (4e–5a).

S: By Zeus, Euthyphro, do *you* really think you know so precisely how the divine stands with reference to piety and impiety, the facts being as you describe them, that you do not fear it is *you* who may stumble into committing an impious act, acting as you do in prosecuting your father?

E: I would be worthless, Socrates, and Euthyphro would in no way be superior to the majority of men, if I did not know all such things with perfect precision.

It surely looks to Socrates, ignorant as *he* is on these matters, that Euthyphro himself is running the risk of committing a hugely impious act, the prosecution of his own father in such ambiguous circumstances.[1] No, Euthyphro must possess the "clear and certain mental apprehension" that knowledge brings regarding the nature of piety and impiety in order to be doing what he is doing. "If you did not know clearly what the pious and the impious were, you would never have undertaken to prosecute your old father for murder on behalf of the dead man, but from fear of the gods you would refuse to run the risk of not acting rightly and being ashamed before men" (15d).

As it is, Socrates's having chanced upon someone with such clear knowledge of the pious and the impious turns out once again to be a fortunate occurrence, because the charge of impiety is precisely one of the charges on which he stands accused. To introduce novel and strange gods into one's city is indeed an impious act, impious towards the gods themselves and impious toward one's own city, one's fatherland. Since Euthyphro must have knowledge of what is pious and what is impious, and since Socrates is charged with having committed serious acts of impiety, Socrates not unreasonably believes Euthyphro can be of great help to him. By Euthyphro's teaching *him* the nature of piety and impiety, Socrates will in turn be able to respond with knowledge and expertise to the charge of impiety brought by his accusers. "So tell me, then, what do you say the pious and the impious are" (5d).

What follows in the dialogue is (unsurprisingly) a spectacle painful to behold. Socrates works his "wizardry" as easily on Euthyphro as he did on Meno. In fact, Euthyphro begins by making

1. *Impious* (adj.): "Wanting in natural reverence and dutifulness, esp. to parents."

the same mistake Meno himself made, though we omitted it in our earlier treatment of the *Meno*. Both Euthyphro and Meno fail to understand what Socrates is asking them. They think Socrates is looking for an example or an instance of a particular kind of act, and Euthyphro's first response to Socrates's question is: "I say that the pious is just what I am doing now, prosecuting the wrongdoer, whether for murder or the theft of sacred objects, or anyone misbehaving in such ways, whether the wrongdoer happens to be your father or your mother or anyone else, and not prosecuting is impious" (5de). Well and good, but Socrates wants to know what piety and impiety are in themselves; he wants a definition as a standard by which to judge whether any given act is in fact pious or impious. Euthyphro's prosecution of his own father may very well indeed be a pious act, but Socrates wants to know just what it is about Euthyphro's conduct that makes it pious (6d–7a).

> S: Remember, I did not ask you to show me one or two instances of the many pious actions but the very form [*eidos*] itself by virtue of which all pious things are pious.... Teach me then this form [*idea*] itself, what it is, so that looking to it and using it as a paradigm, I might say about whatever you or anyone else does, that if it is such it is pious, but if not such, not.
>
> E: But if that is what you want, Socrates, that is what I will tell you.
>
> S: Yes, that is what I want.
>
> E: Well then, what is dear to the gods is pious, what is not dear is impious.
>
> S: Splendid, Euthyphro! What I was looking for you to answer, you have now answered. Whether truly, that I do not know yet, but you will show me plainly that the things you say are true.
>
> E: Certainly.

Ah, yes, whether what Euthyphro says is true. But first, there may be just a few tiny little points to be straightened out. For instance, according to the Greek poets who were popularly thought to be either descendants of the gods or in some way inspired by them, the gods do not always agree with one another. Indeed, they can get into some truly horrific fights among themselves and sometimes even drag poor mortals into their spats. So, we have situations where what is dear to some of the gods is hateful to others. What are we to think in such cases; the same act is both pious (because dear to some of the gods) and impious (because hated by others)? And pushing the question one step further: what are the gods disagreeing about? Would it not likely be about whether some given act was pious or impious, some of the gods thinking the act was pious and therefore loving it, others thinking it impious and therefore hating it? And it will not help us one bit if we define the pious as what *all* the gods love and the impious as what *all* the gods hate. The reason is that we have two pairs of terms—*pious* and *what all the gods love*, *impious* and *what all the gods hate*. The question is, which in each pair comes first? Is an act pious *because* all the gods love it, or is it that all the gods love it *because* the act is pious? And, is an act impious because all the gods hate it, or do all the gods hate it because it is impious? Socrates is raising a fundamental question regarding the *order of intelligibility or causality*. For each pair the question is: which is the more fundamental term, the term which serves to account for and ground the other?

We have seen Socrates searching for definitions in both the *Gorgias* and the *Meno*. Aristotle reports (*Metaphysics* 987b1–3) that Socrates was in fact the first to search for definitions because he was the first to realize their importance, to recognize that in the order of understanding definitions come first; they provide us with the foundation for understanding everything else. If we knew what oratory is, its definition, we would be in a position to know oratory's worth. If we knew what virtue is, we would be in a position to know how virtue might be acquired. If we knew what piety is, we would be in a position to say which acts are pious and which are impious.

In order to explain this concept of "priority in the order of intelligibility" to Euthyphro, Socrates introduces two additional pairs of terms to illustrate the absolutely crucial point he is trying to make: carried and carrier, led and leader. Which is it: (1) is a thing carried because there is a carrier, or is there a carrier because something is carried? (2) Is a thing led because there is a leader, or is there a leader because something is led? (3) Is an act loved by the gods because it is (thought by them to be) pious, or is it pious because the act is loved by the gods? Since a definition contains what is most essential or fundamental to the thing, and because Euthyphro has offered a modified version of the pious in terms of all the gods loving it, then, if he is correct, it is all the gods loving an act which accounts for and explains the act's piety, which constitutes and *is* the act's piety. But can this be right? Is it not rather the case that the gods love an act because they recognize it to be pious (10d)?

> S: What then do we say about the pious, Euthyphro? According to your account, is it not anything other than being loved by all the gods?
>
> E: Yes.
>
> S: *Because* it is pious or because of something else?
>
> E: No, it is because of this.
>
> S: So, it is loved because it is pious. But not pious because it is loved.
>
> E: Apparently.
>
> S: On the other hand, because it is loved by the gods, it is therefore beloved and dear to the gods.
>
> E: Of course.
>
> S: So the dear-to-the-gods is not identical with the pious, Euthyphro, nor the pious identical with the dear-to-the-gods, as you maintain, but the one is different from the other.

In fact we have three different ideas—(1) an act's being pious, (2) the gods loving the act, and (3) the act's being dear to (loved by) the gods. It is (1) that accounts for (2), and (2) that accounts for (3). It is *because* (the gods recognize that) an act is pious that the gods love it. And it is *because* the gods love an act that the act is loved by the gods (and not the other way around).

Concepts (1) and (3) are first of all not identical, not the same; and, second, (1) is more fundamental than and explanatory of both (2) and (3). Furthermore, (3) cannot be the correct definition of (1) for two reasons. First, (3) and (1) are not the same, whereas a correct definition is and must be the same thing as the thing defined. Second, (1) accounts for or explains (3), whereas a correct definition is not accounted for or explained by anything else about the thing. The correct definition of a thing, its *logos*, *is* the thing's account (11bc).

> E: But Socrates, I am unable to tell you what I think. Whatever we have asserted somehow ever circles around us and refuses to remain where we set it.
>
> S: The statements you have made, Euthyphro, are like the works of my ancestor Daedalus. If it were I who had asserted and proposed them, perhaps you would make a joke about me, that because of my genealogical connection with Daedalus the things I construct in words also run off and refuse to remain where someone has placed them. As it is, because these assertions are yours, we are in need of some other joke, though they refuse to remain in place for you, as you yourself can see.

Socrates observes that he is one up on his ancestor. Daedalus could only give his own productions the power of moving about, whereas Socrates is able to bestow that power on the works of others. "And the most exquisite thing about my skill is that I am unwillingly skilled, since I would much rather the arguments remain for me and unmoving stand fast than possess, in addition to the skill of Daedalus, the wealth of Tantalus" (11de).

Socrates calls upon Euthyphro one last time to assist him in his search. "As you are the younger, so are you no less the wiser, but I also say that you are soft from your wealth of wisdom. So now, blessed as you are, exert yourself" (12a). Euthyphro responds, one last time, saying that "the holy and the pious is that part of justice concerned with service of the gods" (12e). Euthyphro's answer is not a bad one; it would explain what we saw earlier. First we have an act that is pious; therefore the gods love it; therefore it is loved by the gods. The gods would naturally love actions they recognize as pious, that is, actions they recognize as being of service to them. Now things are beginning to make sense. And yet, there is one little point with which Socrates needs just the tiniest bit of help. This "service" is presumably some sort of care. What sort of care are the gods in need of, the assistance and help which could be offered them by mortals? Well, the offering of sacrifices and duly established rites. Do the gods need these? No, of course not. Do the gods gain anything from these sacrifices? No, of course not. Then why give them these? Because it pleases them (15b–e).

S: So once again it appears that this is the pious, what is dear to the gods.

E: Very much so.

S: Saying that, are you astonished to find your statements not remaining still but walking about? And do you accuse me as the Daedalus who makes them walk about, when you yourself are far more skilled than Daedalus, making them go around in a circle? Or do you not realize that our argument as it wanders about has returned to the same point? ... So what the pious is has to be examined again by us from the beginning. As for me, I will never willingly play the coward until I learn what it is.... And now I know very well you think you know clearly what the pious is and what it is not. Tell me then, O best of Euthyphros! And do not conceal what you think it is!

E: Until another time, Socrates, for I am in something of a hurry now and the time is getting away from me.

And just where is Euthyphro in a hurry to go? Oh yes, to prosecute his father. Anyway, the dialogue ends with Socrates's hopes for knowledge of piety and impiety dashed. Euthyphro sincerely believes he has knowledge of piety and impiety, but Socrates has his doubts, and the reader may share them. Socrates's "wizardry" seems to have had little if any effect on Euthyphro's mind. Does the fact that he turns out to be a rather young man have any bearing on Euthyphro's lack of interest in pursuing the question any further? Socrates, in contrast, declares that he, Socrates, "will never willingly play the coward until I learn." Simply put, Socrates has "fire in the belly" to pursue this question, Euthyphro does not. Why this difference between the two?

4

GORGIAS, *APOLOGY*, *and* IGNORANCE

Good (adj.)—"Gratifying, favorable, advantageous. Corresponding to one's desires; marked by happiness or prosperity; fortunate."

Ignorant (adj.)—"Destitute of knowledge, either in general or with respect to a particular fact or subject; unknowing, uninformed, unlearned."

Wisdom (n.)—"Knowledge (esp. of a high or abstruse kind); enlightenment, erudition, learning; in early use often = philosophy, science."

When we left Gorgias in chapter 1, he was facing an objection brought by Socrates against his definition of oratory. As you may remember, the objection ran something like this. On the one hand, Gorgias claims that his craft, the skill of oratory, is the most admirable and powerful of all abilities, because it is "the ability to persuade with speeches judges and jurors in a law court, councilors in council-chamber, assemblymen in a public assembly, and in any other political gathering" (452e). But when Socrates asks whether this "ability to persuade with speeches" is the ability to teach, the ability to convey knowledge, Gorgias quickly and without strain admits that the opinion or conviction produced by the orator in the minds of the audience is not knowledge at all but only belief, which, as belief, may or may not be true. Yes, but when we have some matter to decide, how a person is to be healed or how a bridge is to be built or how the enemy is to be opposed, "the orator will not advise then, will he?" (455b). We always look for experts, people with knowledge; we are never content with someone who possesses mere ability to persuade, are we? Grant all that Gorgias claims for his skill: the orator, even given his ignorance, will nonetheless emerge victorious in the political arena over his adversary, however knowledgeable and expert that adversary might be. There is still something missing here, though—the blind leading the blind.

Although it is not easy, Socrates at last succeeds in getting Gorgias to admit the need for knowledge, expertise, and truth (459d–460a):

> S: Does the orator happen to be in the same position regarding what is just and unjust, what is admirable and shameful, what is good and bad, as he is about what is healthy and the subjects of the other crafts? These things he does not know—what is good, what is bad; what is admirable, what is shameful; what is just, what is unjust—but having devised mere belief-persuasion about these matters so as to seem, among those who do not know, to know more than the person who actually does know, even though he himself does not know either. *Or rather,* is it not *necessary* that the orator know, and also *necessary* that your student already know about these matters before he comes to learn oratory from you? And if he does not already know, will *you*, the teacher of oratory, teach the student who has come to you *nothing at all* about these matters—that is not your business, after all—and will you make him appear among the multitude to know about these topics though he does not, to appear excellent though he is not? *Or rather, and above all,* would you be *unable* to teach him oratory *unless he first knows the truth about these matters*? How does all this stand, Gorgias? And by Zeus, as you were just now saying you would, unveil oratory and tell forth its power!

G: Well, Socrates, I suppose that if he happens not to know, he will learn these things from me as well.

S: Hold it right there! You have spoken splendidly! If *you* are going to make someone an orator, he *must* know what things are just, what unjust, either before or after, having learned these things from you.

So Gorgias does indeed possess knowledge about the topics of his oratory after all—the just, the admirable, the good, and their opposites. Well, if Gorgias has knowledge and can teach his students about these matters, then he will be able to do the same for Socrates. It is another fortunate occurrence for Socrates, the same kind he encountered in the *Meno* and the *Euthyphro*. Socrates, ignorant as he is about these things, is overjoyed to find someone who claims to possess knowledge and who therefore presumably will be able to teach the ignorant Socrates the truth about matters of such interest to him. Gorgias is unlike Euthyphro, for he will stay in the hunt with Socrates for the remainder of a rather long dialogue, but what needs further consideration is the remarkable contrast between Euthyphro and Socrates. Euthyphro gives up. Perhaps he really must get to the law court at that very moment, perhaps he is embarrassed to be exposed by Socrates's "wizardry," or perhaps he is simply incurious. Socrates, by contrast, declares he will never give up until he knows. Why this difference?

We shall explore three possible explanations, one in this chapter and two in the next. For the first possibility, let us return to the *Gorgias*. At a crucial point in the dialogue, Socrates pauses in his examination to ask a direct question of Gorgias himself (457e–458b):

You seem to me to be now saying things about oratory that do not at all follow from, nor are even consistent with, what you were saying before. But I am afraid to examine you lest you suppose I am speaking against you for the sake of victory and not in order to make our discussion as clear as pos-

> sible. Now if you are the same kind of a person as I, I would gladly question you; if not, then let it be. And what kind of a person am I? One of those who would gladly be refuted if I were to say something untrue, and gladly refute if someone else were to say something untrue, being not at all less pleased whether refuted or refuting, because I count *this* the greater good by the degree to which being released from the greatest evil is a greater good than to release someone else from it. I believe that *nothing is so great an evil for a human being as false belief about the matters we happen to be speaking about now.*

There we have it! *The greatest evil a person can possibly encounter* is to hold false beliefs, to be ignorant, regarding "the matters we happen to be speaking about now," the just, the admirable, the good, and their opposites—the unjust, the shameful, the bad. But is it really ignorance about *this* that is the greatest evil anyone can undergo?

Well, yes, because as we saw in chapter 2, knowledge of the good, knowledge of what is advantageous, is the *only* possession which is *always and everywhere beneficial.* Without the knowledge of how to use some other possession in a way genuinely beneficial, the mere possession of that thing cannot as such be said to be beneficial *at all.* That is why the topics under discussion in the *Gorgias* are so vital: "Most admirable of all is the examination ... of what sort of man one should be and what should he undertake and how far, whether old or young" (487e–488a). The topics discussed in the *Gorgias*, the *Euthyphro*, and in almost all of Plato's early dialogues, the so-called Socratic dialogues, are nothing other than different components of what I referred to in this book's opening "Apology" as the Big Picture—the best kind of life possible for us. Without that knowledge, that expertise, in the light of which we may direct our lives, *nothing else* will or can be of any benefit to us, *at all.*

Socrates recognizes the importance of knowledge generally and the relative worth of different subjects of knowledge. Most important of all is the knowledge of how best to live the kind of life to which we must devote all our efforts. Socrates sees its worth and he desires it with all the intensity of his being. Is it then enough to recognize the vital importance of a particular kind of knowledge in order to seek it? Well, no. Euthyphro would have forthrightly declared the importance of knowledge of the pious and the impious, but he was not much interested in seeking it, was he? What was missing in Euthyphro's case?

The dialogue *Apology* is an excellent place to discover an answer to this last question, to explain the difference between Socrates and Euthyphro. The *Apology* is not strictly a dialogue, though it possesses features of quasi-dialogue; it purports to be a record of Socrates's defense at his trial. We have been moving toward this climactic event since the *Meno* and well before. The *Gorgias*, for instance, contains numerous allusions to Socrates's final trial; it was his destiny toward which his whole life was inexorably moving.

Socrates's defense, presented before an Athenian jury of 501 citizens, is a defense of the manner of his life. There is nothing in the ordinary sense "apologetic" about it. Indeed, as we shall see, Socrates would have taken anything "apologetic" about his defense to be an instance of impiety. On the other hand, while it is clear from the dialogue that most of the Athenian jurymen were not so hostile to Socrates as to want his death, they did want an "apology" and they did want a promise that he would cease and desist from the kind of activity we saw displayed in the *Euthyphro, Meno*, and *Gorgias*. The Athenians could not understand what Socrates was about; their reaction to him was similar to that of Anytus who took Socrates to be gratuitously badmouthing the great Athenian statesmen. But exactly what did Socrates believe he was doing and why was he doing it? The answers to these questions are presented with great force in the *Apology*.

As Socrates tells it, the whole responsibility can be laid at the feet of his dead friend Chaerephon, who once in his temerity (for which he had a reputation) took it upon himself to ask the oracle at Delphi whether anyone was wiser than Socrates, a rather odd question to put to a god. Apollo replied through his priestess—no, no one was wiser. Socrates, as he tells it, was astonished by the god's answer: "What is the god saying, and why does he speak in such riddles? As for myself, I recognize that no wisdom great or small belongs to me. Why then does he speak as he does, presenting me as the wisest of all? Surely he is not lying; that would not be right of him" (21b).

Socrates's solution to his perplexity, after "puzzling it over for some time," was to set himself "with considerable hesitation" to testing the truth of what the god had said by approaching a man who possessed a high reputation for wisdom. Socrates's idea was this. First, find a man with a wisdom greater than his own, and then confront the god, saying, "This one here is wiser than I, but you said I was the wisest" (21c). Socrates reports the results of his experiment (21cd):

> Well then, I gave a thorough examination to [someone Socrates does not name who was active in politics and had a reputation for wisdom], ... but after speaking with him he seemed to me to be a man who appeared wise to many others—and especially to himself—but in fact was not. Then I undertook to show him that although he thought himself wise he was not, and at this I became disliked by him and by many of the bystanders. But on departing I was saying to myself that yes, indeed, I was wiser than he. Probably neither of us knows anything excellent, but he, ignorant as he was, believed himself to know things, whereas I, since I did not know, did not think I knew. So perhaps by this little bit I was indeed wiser than he, since the things I did not know I did not think I knew.

Socrates repeated his experiment several times, and with the same result. He found that each person he examined did not know what he thought he knew and resented Socrates's effort to show him his own ignorance. Furthermore, this resentment toward Socrates was not confined to the person questioned, but was often shared by others. "I sensed, with sorrow and fear, that I was becoming hated, but it seemed necessary to regard the remark of the god as something of great importance.... All my wandering about was a labor undertaken so that the god remain unrefuted in my case" (21e–22a). Socrates began with politicians and statesmen, then turned to the poets, "the makers of tragedies, dithyrambs, and all the rest." (As descendants of the gods or in some way inspired by them, poets were popularly believed to possess a super-human form of wisdom.) He ended by turning his attention to the skilled craftsmen (22de):

> I knew I would find them knowing many lovely things, and in this I was not deceived, for they knew things I did not know, and in this respect were wiser than I. But, men of Athens, the skilled craftsmen seemed to me to make the very same mistake the poets had—because of his ability to employ his craft in an excellent fashion, each thought himself to be thoroughly wise about other important matters, and this mistake on their part eclipsed their genuine wisdom.[1] So I asked myself on behalf of the oracle whether I would prefer to be as I was, neither wise in their wisdom nor ignorant in their ignorance, or possess both as they did. And I answered myself and the oracle that it profited me to be as I was.

This endeavor by Socrates, this task "undertaken so that the god remain unrefuted in my case" (22a), gave rise to "much hostility toward me of a kind most difficult to deal with and very deep,

1. Socrates's comment here provides a particularly nice illustration of the so-called generalization of expertise: the common, unwarranted, and typically unconscious inference from the fact that so-and-so is an acknowledged expert in field A, to the conclusion that he must therefore be an expert in some *tangentially related* field B. For instance, someone who is an expert in investment is therefore taken to be an expert in tax policy. So-and-so may in fact be an expert in both fields, but that he is cannot legitimately be inferred from the fact that he is an expert in either one of them. This error is often made both by the experts themselves and by others.

such that many false accusations have been made by these people, including being called a professional wise man" (23a). The Athenian bystanders, familiar with Socrates's "wandering about," would naturally infer that he, having disproved other people's claims to wisdom, believed himself to possess a great deal of wisdom on those very same topics. Yet this hostility, plausible as it may have been, was based on a misunderstanding and therefore totally unfounded.

Despite the personal costs to Socrates of his "undertaking," it none the less taught him a lesson well worth all the misunderstanding and hostility. It taught him a great truth (23ab):

> It is likely, men [of the Athenian jury], that god in truth is wise, and by this oracle he is saying that human wisdom is worth little or nothing. He seems when he mentions Socrates to be but using my name, citing me as an example, as if he would say, "O men, that man is the wisest who, like Socrates, has come to know that with respect to wisdom he is in truth worthy of nothing."

You cannot look for what you already (think you) have. So, in order to search for something, more is required than the belief that the thing in question is valuable. You have to recognize your own lack, your own worthlessness. Euthyphro surely does believe that knowledge of the pious and the impious is of great importance, but he displays little interest in searching for it. The difference between him and Socrates is that whereas Euthyphro believes he possesses that knowledge, Socrates is certain that he (Socrates) does not.

It bears pointing out here that I can search for knowledge even though I think my beliefs are true regarding a particular question. I can search for knowledge because I recognize its superiority to mere true belief. Knowledge is the reason, the "account" which "fetters" the valuable true belief and prevents it from running off like one of the newly minted sculptures of Socrates's ancestor Daedalus. But being wise is more than having the good luck to hold true beliefs, even if by chance they are willing to "remain and unmoving stand fast" (*Euthyphro* 11d) Being wise requires the "intellectual acquaintance with the fact or truth," the "certain mental apprehension of the truth." And this point suggests something else. We have already noted the value of true beliefs in the possession of more-or-less adequate maps of reality necessary for successful action. But there may be something more here which should not be overlooked and will receive development in the next chapter. In addition to knowledge's practical utility in "binding down" valuable but otherwise slippery true beliefs, knowledge may possess a *worth in itself*. The "certain mental apprehension" of and "intellectual acquaintance" with a fact or truth may be worthwhile even if it has no practical value at all, highly desirable even if it does not provide a basis for any sort of action, successful or otherwise. What could its value be? We will suggest an answer to this question in the following chapter.

And one final point. Just because I believe I am lacking something of great value, does it follow that I will search for it? No, not necessarily. Another requirement must yet be added, something which turns out to be connected with the possibility of knowledge's being worthwhile for its own sake. All of this will be examined in the following chapter, that is, the concluding section of part 1 of this book. Having received its final addition, shall this first part, like one of Daedalus's statues, take on living flesh? Shall it take on life, and how?

5

PHAEDO, *MENO*, *APOLOGY*, *and* REASON

Reason (n.) "That intellectual power or faculty (usually regarded as characteristic of mankind, but sometime also attributed in a certain degree to the lower animals) which is ordinarily employed in adapting thought or action to some end; the guiding principle of the human mind in the process of thinking."

Misanthrope (n.) "A hater of mankind; a man-hater; one who distrusts men and avoids their society."

Misology (n.) "Hatred of reason or discussion; also, hatred of learning or knowledge."

Sin (v.) "To offend against some principle, standard, etc.; to be faulty or wrong."

The account of Socrates's death presented in the *Phaedo* is widely judged to be one of the most moving passages in literature. The dialogue takes its name from the narrator who was present during Socrates's last hours. The reader is expected to know that Socrates's defense at his trial was unsuccessful and that the Athenian jury voted to impose upon him the sentence of death. After a delay of some days, that sentence was carried out. The *Phaedo* reports the events of that last, unforgettable day (57a):

Echecrates: Were you yourself with Socrates, Phaedo, on the day he drank the poison in prison, or did you hear about it from someone else?

Phaedo: I was there myself, Echecrates.

E: What were the things the man said before he died? And how did he die? I would gladly hear about it.

The events of the dialogue are presented to its readers *in memory*.

Socrates's last conversation takes place in the prison where he is to be executed and occurs in the presence of approximately twenty men, most of whom are named. Besides Socrates, the principal figures are two young brothers, Simias and Cebes. Naturally, the dialogue soon turns to the topic of immortality and to a related topic, that of "knowledge as recollection," which incidentally was also developed in the *Meno*. Briefly put, the doctrine of "knowledge as recollection" runs something like this. Where did we get, for instance, the idea of two things being absolutely equal? From the experience of our senses? Well, if we consider things just from our own sense experience, we can recognize that no two things in that experience are *absolutely* equal. They are close to being equal, more or less equal, but not absolutely equal. So where did we get the idea of the absolutely and perfectly equal? Socrates's answer: from our recollecting something we had once known but had forgotten—the idea of the absolutely equal, the form of equality itself.

Suppose I ask you if you know Joe Smith, and you say you do not. I say, "Sure you do," and I show you Joe's picture, and you say, "Oh yes, now I remember him." The picture of Joe is not Joe but it is like Joe, and your seeing the picture of Joe jogs your memory and causes you to remember somebody you did know but had forgotten. Knowing Joe Smith is a recollection of Joe Smith, a recovering of what you once knew but had forgotten. You met Joe Smith ten years ago and then forgot about him, only to have your memory jogged by his picture. But when did you meet the idea of the absolutely equal, the form of equality itself? Not ten years ago, I bet. Then when? Socrates's answer: before you were born. You met all the forms of equality, triangularity, goodness, piety, and virtue before you were born, before your soul was joined with your body. But if knowledge is recollection and your soul (= you) existed before you were born, before you were joined with your body, then you obviously do not need your present body in order to exist, and so there's no reason to believe that death, which is the separation of your soul (= you) from your present body, will bring an end to *you*. And so your soul is immortal and has always been around and has associated with the forms in themselves, but you forgot all about that when you were born or, rather, when your soul was joined to your body. The process of thinking and inquiring and searching for knowledge is the process of recalling to mind what you once knew before birth but have forgotten. This process of thinking and inquiring, this process called "philosophy," is the process of freeing your soul from the burden of forgetting and ignorance with which your soul was loaded down at birth. Philosophy thus can be seen as a "practice of death," a practice of separating soul from body so as to recall to the mind the world of the forms with which you were once at home.

Phaedo, while listing the names of those who were present, remarks in passing that he believed Plato was ill (59b) and therefore not present. Some have taken this remark as a nod to the reader to suggest that the dialogue is not to be taken as a perfectly accurate account of what was said that day. However that may be, we at any rate have something like an argument for the immortality of the soul: knowledge is recollection, and therefore the soul existed before it was united with the body, and therefore the soul will exist when it is no longer united to the body.

However, Cebes has a worry that Socrates's argument from "learning as recollection" does not remove. He introduces the image of a man who has worn out many cloaks in his lifetime. He has worn out first one cloak, then another. The man is obviously much longer-lasting than any one of his cloaks. So, having worn out, let us suppose, six cloaks in his lifetime, he acquires a seventh and wears it a while and then dies. Shall we say that the man still endures because (1) he is much longer-lasting than any cloak and (2) here is his (seventh) cloak, still around? Of course not. You will wear out many pairs of jeans in your lifetime, but there will be one pair of jeans which will, so to speak, "wear you out." So, your soul may have been around long before your body and be much more durable than your body. Your soul may have gone through a series of many incarnations. But no matter how many reincarnations your soul may have gone through, it does not follow that this present incarnation, this present joining of your soul to a body, will not be your last. What has happened in the past to your soul and the body to which it was once joined cannot be a certain guide to what will happen to your soul when it and this present body of yours cease to be joined. When Cebes brought out this argument, everyone around Socrates was stunned (88c).

P: Having heard this argument we were all greatly distressed, as we remarked to one other afterwards, because we had been very much persuaded by the previous argument of Socrates, and now this new argument seemed to confuse us once again, and to hurl us into disbelief not only regarding what had already been said *but also regarding what was going to be said,* a fear that none of us was an adequate judge of anything, or that the question itself was unresolvable.

The really disturbing possibility, as Phaedo sees it, is not so much that Socrates and his friends might have been mistaken about the *conclusion* of the argument from "knowledge as recollection," that the soul might turn out not to be immortal after all. What seems to Phaedo and the others to have been put at risk by Cebes is the reliability of *argument as such*. Even Echecrates who is hearing this second-hand is shaken by Phaedo's report. "By the gods, Phaedo, I have the same feeling as yours, for as I listened to you just now the same thought occurred to me, 'Upon what argument can we still rely, for the argument Socrates presented was extremely convincing but has now collapsed in doubt?'" (88cd).

The reader has had this experience, I am sure—listening to some argument and finding it highly persuasive and then hearing some objection to it which you find devastating. Each position sounds compelling until you listen to the first objection which overthrows the position, only to discover that the counter-response demolishes the objection, etc. What lesson do we take away from this? And what lesson did Socrates take away (88d–89c)?

E: So tell me then, by Zeus, how Socrates confronted the objection and whether he became, as you said all of you did, obviously upset, or not, but calmly came to the aid of his argument, and was his assistance sufficient or did it fall short? Give us an account of everything as precisely as you can!

P: Well, Echecrates, I have on many occasions marveled at Socrates, but never was I more astonished by him than at that moment. That he had an answer was perhaps not at all out of the ordinary. But what especially amazed me about him was this: first, how kindly and graciously and admiringly he received the young men's objection, and then how acutely he sensed how affected we were by the objection, and then how effectively he healed us and, as though we were defeated and fleeing from battle, called us back and turned us around to follow at his side and join with him in examination of the objection.

E: How?

P: I will tell you. By chance I was to his right sitting on a low stool next to his couch, so he was well above me. He touched my head and squeezed together the hair on my neck; he was accustomed to play with my hair on occasion. "Tomorrow," he said, "you will perhaps cut this lovely hair, Phaedo" [that is, as a sign of mourning].

"Very likely, Socrates," I said.

"Not at all if you will follow my advice."

"But why?" I said.

"Today," he said, "I shall cut my hair and you yours should the argument die on us and we are unable to bring it back to life. If I were you and the argument fled from me, I would swear an oath as the Argives did not to let my hair grow long before I had won the victory, battling against Cebes's objection."

Before attempting to restore his argument to life, Socrates warns us that "we should take care lest something happen to us" (89de):

> Let us not become misologues, as people become misanthropes. *There is no greater evil one can suffer than the hatred of reason*. Misology and misanthropy arise in the same manner. Misanthropy insinuates itself when someone lacking skill has placed total confidence in another person and takes him to be truthful in every way and sound and a man worthy of trust; and then, a little while later, he discovers he is rotten and unfaithful, and this happens in another instance; and when someone has had this experience on a number of occasions and in particular with those he thought his close associates and companions, finally, after encountering many such, he hates everyone and thinks that no one ever is sound in any way. Have you not yourself seen this happening?

Misanthropy's inference from "some people have mistreated me" to the conclusion that "no one is to be trusted" is obviously a totally unwarranted inference. The truth, as Socrates sees it, is that "the good and the bad, each of them are very few, most are somewhere in between" (90a). Most people indeed do have some bad in them and some people may have quite a lot; but to say that all are totally bad is plainly mistaken on its face. And besides that, misanthropy is "something shameful and clearly arises when someone who lacks skill in human affairs but nevertheless undertakes dealings with other humans. If he did possess that skill, he would recognize what is in fact the case" (89e). The explanation for misanthropy lies not with the behavior of other people but within the misanthrope himself. What he is doing is trying to shift blame from himself to others. It is *he* who is responsible because of his ignorance.

Something analogous can be said of anyone who has a complete distrust or dislike for all argument. Some arguments are good, some bad. The person with skill in argumentation will be able to detect a bad argument when it appears. If he is fooled by some bad argument, he will not blame the argument but rather himself for being fooled by it. In contrast (90bc):

> When someone places confidence in an argument as reliable, but does so without skill in reasoned argumentation, he may a little later come to believe that the same argument is bad, as sometimes it is and sometimes not, and then in turn with another argument and then another. You of course know about those who spend a lot of their time with arguments opposed to other arguments, how they wind up thinking *they* have become the wisest of the wise and *only they* have realized that nothing is sound or stable in any object or in any argument, but that all things that are float, now up and now down, and for no length of times does anything remain the same in any respect.

Like the misanthrope, there is something wretched about the misologue (90c–e):

> S: This experience would be worthy of pity, Phaedo, if indeed there did exist an argument that was true and reliable and able to be understood thoroughly, and if a man, because he had in the past dealt with arguments that sometimes appear true and sometimes not, should blame neither himself nor his own lack of skill but should wind up, because of his discomfort, quite happily shifting blame away from himself to the arguments, and spend the remaining part of his life hating and speaking badly of reasoned discourse, *and so be rendered barren of the truth and the knowledge of things.*
>
> P: Yes, by Zeus, *that would surely be worthy of pity.*
>
> S: So this is the first thing we must be careful about. We should not allow to slip into our minds the suspicion that nothing about argumentation is sound, but quite to the contrary that it is we who are not yet sound so that *courage and zeal to become sound are what are called for.*

I will not search for a thing if I believe I do not possess the resources necessary to find it. If I have lost my ring at the bottom of a pool that is fifteen feet deep, I am not going to waste my time paddling around on the surface when I know I do not have the swimming and diving skills to reach the bottom. Similarly, if I believe that something can be discovered only by reason but I have no confidence in reason's powers because I "have become the wisest of the wise and only I have realized that nothing is sound or stable in any object or in any argument," I will not even begin the search for it, thinking that the endeavor is nothing but a fool's game which I and a few others who are among the wisest like me have seen through.

Reasoning correctly is not a fool's game, but as we shall see, it is not child's play, either. It demands a set of skills, elements of which will constitute the focus of part 2 of this book. Though it is not always easy to distinguish good arguments from bad ones, the distinction between them is real and can be drawn with considerable confidence. Arguments in their actual employment range from excellent to extremely poor, with every grade in between. It can therefore be difficult in a particular case to decide whether to call the argument good or bad, but the person who says that there are no good arguments, at all, that all reasoning is bad or unreliable—the misologue—displays by his own words that he "lacks skill" in logic and the process of reasoning. We'll have something more to say about misology in chapter 7.

In order to search for the truth, it must be the case that the searcher believes he has the tools necessary to conduct that search. If the inquiry is to be carried out by the exercise of one's reason, the searcher must have an *appropriate* level of confidence in reason. He must be aware of and on the lookout for reason's limits and pitfalls, know how far reason can take him and where it reaches its limits. Like a loaded weapon, reason must be employed with respect and care. Naïve over-confidence in reason's powers is a sin against reason, but so is misology, and each is also a sin against the rational animal himself.

To examine this final point, it will help if we return first to the *Meno* and then to the *Apology*. The *Meno*, we recall, opens abruptly with Meno's ordering Socrates to tell him how virtue is acquired, whether it can be taught or developed by practice or possessed at birth or acquired in some other way. Incidentally, this subject was one of much fascination to the Greeks; they were always discussing it and everyone had his own opinion about it. Meno is therefore asking for just one more opinion on a topic about which he knew of a dozen opinions or more. Remember also Socrates's response: he could not answer the question and had no opinion on the subject because he did not know what virtue was and had never even met anyone who did know. Meno finds Socrates's last remark literally incredible, but after the exercise of Socrates's "wizardry," Meno is driven to admit that he too has not a clue about the nature of virtue.

So Socrates does not know what virtue is and neither, it seems, does Meno. Far from giving up, Socrates performs the characteristic act of calling upon Meno not to give up either but to continue the search for the nature of virtue together with him. Meno demurs (80d–81a):

> M: But in what way will you search for this thing, Socrates, when you have absolutely no idea what it is? What sort of a target can you propose for your search when you do not know anything about it? And even if you did happen to hit upon it, how would you know that *this* is that which you did not know?
>
> S:... Do you recognize what an eristic [that is, "adapted for or disposed to controversy"] argument you bring up, how there is nothing a man can search for, neither what he knows nor what he does not know? He cannot search for what he knows—he knows it, so there is no point for the search—nor for what he does not know, because he does not know what he is searching for.
>
> M: Doesn't that argument seem well stated to you, Socrates?

S: Not to me.
M: Can you explain why?
S: I can, for I have heard wise men and women speak of divine matters.
M: What did they say?
S: What was true, it seemed to me, and lovely.

The "divine matters" which Socrates thinks "true and lovely" are the immortality of the soul and its multiple reincarnations, multiple joinings with a body, sometimes human and sometimes not. In the process of this presentation of "divine matters," Socrates introduces a celebrated argument for the doctrine of "learning as recollection." We have already provided a sketch of that doctrine and a further elaboration of it would not be to the purpose here, but what is very much to the point is the lesson Socrates draws from his argument (86bc):

S: Well, if the truth of things is forever in our soul, the soul would be deathless, and therefore there is need for courage regarding what you at present happen not to be knowing—that is, what you are not remembering. So, undertake the search, and remember!

M: These things seem to me to have been well said, Socrates, though I do not know how.

S: And to me as well, Meno. On the other points of the argument I would not stubbornly hold fast, but on this I do: believing we must search for what we do not know, we will be better and more courageous and less good-for-nothings than if we believe that what we do not know can be neither discovered nor is something to be searched for—for the sake of this I would do battle with everything I had, both in word and in deed.

Why is this so? Why are we the worse for not engaging in this search for the knowledge we do not possess and that may not even exist? The vehemence with which Socrates asserts his belief shows it to have been at the core of his being. This same insistence on the absolute necessity of the search reappears at the end of Socrates's trial, as reported in the *Apology*. Socrates has been found guilty, and his accusers have asked for the penalty of death. It is now up to Socrates to propose an alternative penalty (37e–38b):

> Perhaps someone might say, "But Socrates, having departed from us [into exile] would you not be able to live in silence and at rest?" And it is just this that is the most difficult of all things to persuade some of you. Even if I say doing what you ask would be disobeying the god and therefore I *cannot* remain at peace, you would still not believe me as someone who is merely being ironical. And if I in turn say that *this* is the greatest good that can befall a man—each day to examine arguments regarding virtue and the other things about which you hear me discussing and examining both myself and others, for *the unexamined life is not to be lived by a man*—you will believe me even less if I say that. But these things are as I say them to be, gentlemen, but to persuade you is by no means easy.

As we pointed out before, many of the members of the jury were not personally hostile to Socrates, but they very much did want him to shut up and stop practicing his "wizardry." And that was precisely what Socrates claimed he absolutely could not do, and he offered two reasons, one personal, one impersonal. The personal reason is that he believed he had a direct mandate from the god to conduct this search for someone wiser than he. But the second, impersonal reason applies to us all—*the greatest good any of us can possibly engage in is the constant search for the knowledge of virtue, justice, the good, and the admirable*, for without this constant search, this examination of oneself and one's life, the life we do lead is *not to be lived* by us.

At the end of the previous chapter we returned to the importance of knowledge and suggested that although knowledge has great practical utility because it "binds down" or "fetters" by an account or reason the true belief necessary for successful action, the possession of knowledge may also possess a worth in and of itself, separate from its obvious utility. And what might this intrinsic worth be? Recall the definition of "reason" presented above: "That intellectual power or faculty, usually regarded as characteristic of mankind, which is ordinarily employed in adapting thought or action to some end." Recall also Socrates's remark that we will be better human beings if we engage in the search for knowledge. Recall, finally, the definition most of us picked up somewhere along the way of "man" as "rational animal." We will be better men, better rational animals, if we use the reason that is ours by nature, the reason that defines us, if we try to adapt our thought and action to the most important of ends, the end of living the best life we can possibly live. The search for knowledge by the use of our reason has its manifest practical usefulness, but also and more fundamentally it has a worth that is intrinsic to itself. Reasoning is what we do, it makes us what we are and makes us better insofar as we engage well in it. In contrast, to reject the use of reason *in contexts where its use is appropriate* is to reject the core power of the rational animal and thus to demean the self that possesses this power. In this regard, we might also reflect upon the scientific name for our species, *Homo sapiens*, "wise man." Again, the search for wisdom, enlightenment, science, and deep understanding is the practice which defines us as human beings; it makes us who we are. We do not need an external justification for engaging in the search for knowledge and understanding and wisdom.

In order to search for something, it is necessary that one regard the search itself as worthwhile, but the worthiness of the search can have either (or both) of two components. First, it may be worth while because the search is likely to pay off, because the thing we are searching for is something we may be able to discover through our search. But the second possibility is that the search is worthwhile in and of itself; like the act of loving, even if we do not find that for which we are searching, we will be better for having searched and failed than never to have searched at all. Whether or not our reasoning achieves its goal, if we have reasoned well, we have done well and we are the better and more excellent for it.

CONCLUSION *to* PART 1

Lessons to Be Drawn

Since it is possible that we have forgotten where we are going, where we have been, and where we are, let us return to the opening "Apology" to reset our bearings. The study of ethics—the examination of the best life we can possibly live and the means to live such a life—will be seen by many as a pointless and worthless exercise because there does not seem to be any truth about the matter. And the reason there appears to be no truth about the topic of ethics is that there appears to be no general consensus about it. If there were indeed real truth about ethical matters, we would expect to find at least some degree of consensus. Finding no consensus whatever, one infers that there is no truth about ethics to be discovered. Now the absence of any general consensus is obvious if one counts everybody who has any opinion at all on ethical topics. But in the case of the natural sciences, when we search for the existence of some general consensus, we do not look for such consensus among all those who happen to have an opinion on scientific matters. No, we take into account the opinions only of those whom we believe to be "qualified researchers" on the topic and look for a consensus only among *them*.

The expression "qualified researcher" refers to those people who possess whatever traits we recognize as necessary or helpful for acquiring truth about the topic at hand. For instance, we might imagine a group of some hundred researchers, fifty of whom hold one opinion and fifty of whom hold a different opinion on some scientific topic. No consensus exists among the hundred researchers. But if we were to ask the question of who among the hundred is a qualified researcher, we might find that only six of them are, and discover further that those six all share the same opinion on the topic. Thus, there would be no consensus among the researchers as such, but unanimity among the qualified researchers. The lack of consensus in the first count would bear no significance for us who are concerned with the truth, but the fact of consensus in the second count would be highly relevant.

Thus the distinction between qualified and unqualified researchers in any field is a matter of the first importance for anyone concerned about the truth regarding that subject. And so it should be for the field of ethics. The absence of widespread consensus about ethics would be significant if that absence were to be found among qualified researchers, but it would convey nothing of importance if the group were composed mostly of unqualified researchers. So the question is: (1) is this lack of consensus a lack among qualified or unqualified researchers? And this question leads to two others: (2) just what are the traits that make a researcher qualified, and (3) is it question-begging to declare what those traits are?

The thrust of this book is to provide a resoundingly negative answer to (3) and to provide a list of such traits in response to (2). A person does not need to possess a proposed trait of a qualified researcher in ethics in order to recognize the proposed trait as indeed such a trait. This last assertion can only be supported by acting on it, and this is precisely what this conclusion to part 1 sets out to do. Remember the test: in order for a proposed trait to be included among the traits of a qualified researcher (the expression "qualified researcher" will be specified by the list of traits), it is necessary that *everyone* agree that the trait does indeed belong to any qualified researcher, and this "everyone" must include *even those who lack the trait in question*.

First, in order to be a qualified researcher in the field of ethics, one must genuinely and deeply desire to seek for the truth to the degree it can be found. One desires this search because one believes either that the search *itself* is important, or that the possession of knowledge may be of great value, or both. Does not this condition seem right, even to those who do not much care about the truth? If one is going to be a qualified researcher in the field of ethics (or in any other field for that matter), one needs to have a desire to seek for and find the truth. People who care about baseball are more likely to know the scores of last night's games than those who do not care. Winners mostly come from the ranks of those who want to win.

Second, in order to possess a desire to seek for and acquire the truth, and therefore in order to be a qualified researcher in the field of ethics, it is necessary that one believe that such a truth might exist. It is *not* necessary that one believe that there *is* such a truth, only that there *might* be. Is this not obvious even for those who are sure there is no such a thing as truth in ethics? Okay, there is no truth, but *if* there were, would not the ones best positioned to find it be those who believe there *might* be something there to be found? I myself do not believe that any American or Israeli conspiracy brought down the Twin Towers, but *if* there were such a conspiracy, it is clear even to me that those who believe there *might* have been such a conspiracy have a big advantage over me in uncovering it.

Third, in order to possess a desire to search for and acquire the truth, and therefore in order to be a qualified researcher in the field of ethics, it is necessary to believe that one might not yet possess the truth in all of its depth and in all of its ramifications. Someone might think that he does not possess the truth at all, that he is totally ignorant, or he might believe that he is pretty sure of being generally right but might none the less lack full knowledge—that he might not yet possess the full, clear, and certain mental apprehension of the truth of his belief. Would not this seem right even to someone who is confident he does know everything that could be known about the subject of ethics? How can I be a qualified researcher if I see no reason for me to do the research? If I watched a game last night to its finish, I am not going to turn on the radio to get the score.

Fourth, in order to possess a desire to search for and acquire the truth, and therefore in order to be a qualified researcher in the field of ethics, it is necessary to believe that the truth, if it exists, is something that might be discovered by the method appropriate to the field of ethics, by the correct exercise of reason. It is not necessary to believe that the truth *will* be discovered but that it *might* be. Would not this fourth point seem obvious even to someone who disbelieves in the power of reason generally or at least in its use in the field of ethics? If I do not trust reason, why would I ever become a researcher in the field of ethics, which field by its nature conducts its examination through the exercise of reason? If I do not believe in dowsing or water-witching, why would I ever (except perhaps for the sheer amusement) pick up a forked branch, hold it level, and begin walking over a plot of ground? People who do not believe in horoscopes do not consult them to decide if today is their lucky day.

The field of ethics is ultimately all about the Big Picture, an account of the very best kind of life one can possibly live. Some people believe there is no truth to be had about the topic (because of the argument from unresolved widespread disagreement or for other reasons). Some have no desire to gain knowledge about the subject either because they see no possible value in the possession of ethical truth or because they are simply incurious. Some are certain they already know whatever they need to know about the topic. And some doubt reason's power and worth, either generally or specifically with regard to ethics. A person fitting into one of the four categories may not see himself as falling under the category, even after it is fully explained. People who are *generally* incurious (in contrast to being uninterested in a given topic) do not see themselves as incurious. The category of "incurious" makes sense only to people who do not belong to it. It is quite frequently extraordinarily difficult to see ourselves as we truly are.

Let us summarize our results thus far. In order to be a qualified researcher in the field of ethics, the possession of each of the following traits is necessary: a strong desire to search for the truth about the Big Picture; a belief that truth regarding the Big Picture *may* exist; a belief that the possession of knowledge regarding the Big Picture *may* be of great value or that the search for it is something important in its own right; a belief that the researcher himself *may* lack full knowledge of the truth regarding the Big Picture; and a belief that truth regarding the Big Picture *may* be discovered and knowledge gained by the correct exercise of reason. Do you see yourself as possessing all of these traits? Might they become enfleshed, alive? The next time you are in a discussion about moral topics, you might do well to ask the person with whom you are speaking whether *he* sees himself as possessing all five traits. You might be unpleasantly surprised by the person's answer. And then what do you do?

In both the second and the third parts of this book further traits will be discovered and added as necessary traits for any qualified researcher in the field of ethics. The rough division marked by these two parts is that part 2 stresses cognitive or intellectual traits, while part 3 focuses on what may be called "moral" traits or features of desire. For both the test to be met is the same as the one insisted upon and employed here: in order to be entered into our list of necessary traits for any qualified observer, a given trait must be recognized as such by all, even by those who lack the trait in question. When we have completed parts 2 and 3, we will conduct a final review and summary in order to appreciate fully what accompanying Socrates in his search has gained for us.

PART 2

THE SEARCH *for* TRUTH *and* *the* GOOD DIALECTICIAN

6

GORGIAS, *PROTAGORAS*, *and* DIALECTIC

Four Traits of the Good Dialectician

Dialectic (n.) "The art of critical examination into the truth of an opinion; the investigation of truth by discussion."

Bombast (v.) "To stuff, swell out, inflate; to render grandiose (a speech or literary composition) with bombastic language."

When we left off our treatment of the *Gorgias* in chapter 4, Socrates was asking Gorgias about the kind of person he took himself to be (457e–458a):

You seem to me to be now saying things about oratory that do not at all follow from, nor are even consistent with, what you were saying before. But I am afraid to examine you lest you suppose I am speaking against you for the sake of victory and not in order to make our discussion as clear as possible. Now if you are the same kind of a person as I, I would most gladly question you; if not, then let it be. And what kind of a person am I? One of those who would gladly be refuted if I were to say something untrue, and gladly refute if someone else were to say something untrue, being not at all less pleased whether refuted or refuting.

The "examination" to which Socrates refers is, as we saw, nothing other than a search for knowledge of the very best kind of life one can possibly lead. "Most admirable of all is the examination ... of what sort of man one should be and what should he undertake and how far, whether old or young" (487e–488a). And this search, for Socrates, must take the form of collaboration, a *joint* undertaking with the assistance of genuine *partners*. On the other hand, Socrates is well aware that many if not most discussions turn out to be of quite a different character. He prefaces his question to Gorgias with this remark (457c–e):

> I believe, Gorgias, you have experienced, as I have, many arguments and have observed in them this feature: the participants find it not at all easy to define for each other the subject they have undertaken to examine, and then *having learned from and taught one other*, to end the meeting. Rather, if they dispute some point and one claims that the other is incorrect or unclear, they get angry and believe the other is speaking from malice, becoming eager to win rather than investigating the topic under discussion. It can happen that, finishing up, they leave one another in a most shameful manner, being reviled and saying and hearing such things about themselves that even the bystanders are annoyed with themselves for having thought it worthwhile to become listeners of such people.

I think each one of us has, in one way or another, been in this position. Warranted or unwarranted, misology is an easily explicable phenomenon and there are all too many opportunities to acquire and develop it.

In contrast, the practice of argument and discussion and examination is first and foremost an inquiry not into the *persons* holding a position but into the *truth* of the position itself. It is *not* a striving to win, which must be a zero-sum game with at least one loser for every winner. Rather, it is an activity with *multiple* winners—*all* those who participate as genuine partners in the search for truth. Who refutes ("wins") and who is refuted ("loses") matters not. Indeed, as we saw Socrates assert in chapter 4, "I count this the greater good by the degree to which being released from the greatest evil is a greater good than to release someone else from it. I believe that nothing is so great an evil for a human being as false belief about the matters we happen to be speaking about now" (458a). This practice of argument, discussion, examination, what we will call "dialectic," is, as we have seen, the activity of raising pointed, incisive questions designed to throw light on the topic at hand. The first trait of the good dialectician, then, is *knowledge of the questions to be asked and the order in which to ask them.*

Let us return to the discussion of the *Gorgias* in order to provide another illustration of how this question-putting is supposed to work. Recall that Socrates understands the dialogue to be a part of what is "the most admirable of all," a search into the question of "what sort of man one should be and what should he undertake and how far." Its particular topic, the nature of oratory and its worth, is simply one feature of Socrates's more general, universal search. How far, if we are to live an excellent life, must we devote ourselves to the acquisition and practice of oratory? If there is any truth about the Big Picture, to what extent will it—must it—incorporate (or exclude) oratory?

In addition to Socrates and Gorgias, both older seasoned men, the dialogue involves two other principal speakers, both young—Polus, a professional student and practitioner of oratory, and Callicles, a man just beginning his career in politics. Callicles may not have received any formal training in oratory, but Gorgias is staying at Callicles's house and is highly sympathetic to the craft, taking Socrates to task for turning away from the practice of oratory in order to devote his life exclusively to the practice of philosophy. Callicles makes the strongest charge that can be brought against any proposed Big Picture, stating that by devoting himself exclusively to philosophy instead of practicing oratory and engaging in political affairs, *Socrates is wasting his life* (485e–486b):

> You are paying no attention, Socrates, to the things you should be concerned about, and although your soul's nature is excellent, you assume the pose of a mere youth.... And so, if someone should seize you or anyone else like you and drag you to prison alleging you had acted unjustly, though you had done no such thing, know well that you would not be of any use to yourself. Your head would spin, your mouth hang open, with nothing to say in return. Having entered the courtroom and encountering some completely worthless rascal of an accuser, you would be put to death, if death was what he wanted to punish you with. But how can this be something wise, Socrates, this craft [philosophy] which, having taken hold of a man with natural ability, made him worse, able neither to help himself nor save himself or anyone else from the gravest of dangers, to be stripped of all his possessions by his enemies, and to live a life without resource or respect in his city?

Later in the dialogue Callicles offers a similar warning, to which Socrates responds (511bc):

> S: I do know that, my excellent Callicles, if I am not deaf, and I hear you say it, Polus just now saying it many times, and nearly everybody else in this city. But now you listen to me, too: yes he may kill me if he so desires, but it would be a bad man killing a good one.
>
> C: And is this not what is most infuriating?
>
> S: No, not for a person of intelligence.... Or do you believe that a man should focus on this: how to live as long as possible and pay attention to those crafts that are always there to rescue us from dangers, such as the one you call on me to practice, oratory which preserves us in the law courts?
>
> C: Yes, by Zeus, and in doing so I advise you well.
>
> S: Really, my excellent friend? And does the skill of swimming seem to you something majestic?
>
> C: No, by Zeus, not to me.

Why does Socrates ask such an absurd, off-topic question? Because it is not off topic at all. If oratory is a noble and honorable craft because it protects its possessor from the risk of being (unjustly) punished or killed, then other crafts which protect their possessors from dying prematurely should receive similar praise. Does not the craft of swimming protect its possessor from the untimely death of drowning? And if it does, is it not worthy of the same praise Callicles bestows upon oratory? Socrates mentions two other crafts, piloting ships and engineering, both of which possess the same life-protecting feature possessed by oratory and swimming. Are they not also worthy of praise and esteem? Regarding the engineer (*mêchanopoión*, literally "maker of machines"), Socrates remarks (512b–d):

> If he wished to say, Callicles, the sort of things you people say, showing the majesty of his craft, showering you with his speeches, orating and encouraging you about how necessary it was to become engineers because nothing else is worth anything. And the speech would be sufficient to make his point. But *you* look down upon him and think nothing is lower than he and his craft, and reproach him, calling him "engineer," "builder of machines." And you would refuse to give your daughter to his son, or take his daughter for yourself. But from the things you yourself have said, by what fair reason do you look down upon the engineer and the others I mentioned just now?

Callicles is in fact terribly mistaken about the Big Picture (512de):

> Look, see whether what is noble and good is not something different from saving and being saved. Rather, is it not this: to live whatever length of life is allowed as a true man rather than as a clinger-to-life. And having turned over that concern to the god, and having trusted the women who say that no single person escapes fate, he should then concentrate on one thing only, the manner by which he might live the remaining part of his life in as excellent a way as possible.

If the art and practice of oratory is noble and excellent because it offers protection from death and other losses, why do not other arts and crafts which provide similar protection receive similar praise from Callicles? And it is therefore now up to Callicles to explain why oratory retains its status as an admirable craft in contrast to the others, in spite of the fact that they are all equally life-preserving.

The first trait of the good dialectician, the ability to discover and raise discussion-advancing questions in an appropriate order, is closely related to a second and more general trait, *knowledge of logical entailments*. In order to ask Callicles the question he does, Socrates must recognize this: "If a thing A (oratory) is B (admirable) *because* it is C (life-preserving), then a different thing D (swimming), which is also C, *should* also be B as well, and for the very same reason." It could turn out, of course, that D is *not* B *in spite of its being* C; but if so, then something *else* needs to be added to explain why D is not B while A is. Callicles can claim that oratory (A) is admirable (B) while insisting that swimming and engineering (D) are not, even though all of them are life-preserving (C), but he has some work to do.

Callicles understands logical entailment, and his ability causes him considerable discomfort at one point in the dialogue. Callicles had earlier made a remarkable assertion that becomes the focus about which the rest of the dialogue centers (491e–492a,c):

> This is what is admirable and just by nature, what I say to you now with complete openness: the person who is going to live correctly must allow his own appetites to become as great as possible and not to hold them in check; and when they have become as great as possible, he must be competent to serve[1] them with courage and intelligence and to fill them up whenever an appetite arises.... But the truth, Socrates, which you claim to pursue, here it is: luxury and licentiousness and liberty, if held in abundance, this is excellence and happiness.

1. The Greek word primarily means "to row, to serve on board ship," but because the act of rowing is hard work, another meaning of the verb is "to do hard service."

An amazing declaration. Callicles also says that just about everyone would prefer to live a life like this, but most people lack the necessary stuff to pull it off. So, "concealing their own inability," they praise what they know deep down to be shameful, a life of fair-dealing and honesty and moderation and self-control. And maybe Callicles is right about this and most people deep down do agree with him, though perhaps few would be daring enough to admit it. But let us see if Callicles's position will survive Socrates's dialectical questioning as he pursues the logical entailments of this position.

First, notice one important point about Callicles's claim. When he speaks about the appetites (desires, cravings) one should allow to become as large as possible, he does not suggest *any* qualifications or restrictions. Whatever you have an appetite for, let your craving grow as great as possible; do not restrain it in any way, but rather, use your competence and bravery and intelligence to satisfy your craving in a competent fashion, that is, in such a way that you are not caught and punished or in some other way suffer for having acted to gratify your desire. Callicles's recommendation is not for everyone. It is not for those who lack the necessary intelligence and toughness and daring to gratify their cravings without suffering for it in some way. But if you are one of the few who has got what it takes, then go for it without any restriction or limitation on the gratification of your desires!

Perhaps you see yourself as one of the lucky few capable of pulling it off, capable of living the life Callicles recommends. Why does Callicles insist that you allow whatever desires you have to grow as great as possible? Now of course, most people should not do this. Not being able to gratify their longings, they will inevitably experience pain from their frustrated desires, and the stronger their desires the greater their frustrations and the greater their pain. So, for them, they will be well advised to keep their longings few and weak in order to avoid the inevitable consequence of unsatisfied desire. But you who have the rare capacity to "live correctly," in contrast to the many weak and inferior human beings, must allow your desires to grow as great as possible, allow them to rage, to roar, to burn. And why? Because you, the excellent human you are, will not experience ungratified desire. Oh no, you are competent and brave and intelligent and you possess the wherewithal to gratify those desires and to experience the pleasure that comes from their gratification, and the greater the desires the greater the pleasure that comes from gratifying them. Every desire has a strength; the stronger a desire the more painful its frustration but the more pleasant its gratification. So you see now why you should work at growing your desires to become roaring lions; since you are going to gratify them anyway, being the excellent and competent human you are, you will be receiving greater pleasure the more you work at stirring up whatever desires you happen to have. But now what (494b–d)?

> S: Do you say there is such a thing as hunger and eating when one is hungry?
>
> C: Yes.
>
> S: And thirst and drinking when one is thirsty?
>
> C: Yes, and having all the other appetites and being able to fill them up enjoyably and live happily.
>
> S: ... First, say whether someone itching and scratching, having in abundance the ability to scratch, scratching throughout his entire life, is living happily.
>
> C: How absurd you are, Socrates, a sheer grandstander.
>
> S: ... But you are courageous, so just answer.
>
> C: I say, then, that even the one scratching would live pleasantly.
>
> S: And if pleasantly then happily as well?
>
> C: Absolutely.

As if the scratching example were not bad enough, we now have something even more likely to unsettle Callicles (494e–495b):

S: Is it his head alone he will scratch, or is there something still remaining for me to ask you? See, Callicles, what would you answer if someone should ask you all the things following closely upon what you have said? And is not the upshot of all this the life of a catamite [that is, a young boy used for homosexual prostitution], is this not a terrible and shameful and wretched life? Or will you dare to call them happy as long as they have in abundance whatever things they stand in need of?

C: Are you not ashamed, Socrates, bringing the discussion to such matters?

S: But do I bring it here, my splendid friend, or the one who says, thoughtlessly, that those who are enjoying themselves, however they may do so, are happy, and does not distinguish among pleasures which are the good, which the bad? But answer now whether you still say the pleasant and the good are the same, or that some pleasure is not good.

C: Well, in order that my argument not become inconsistent should I say they are different, I will say they are the same.

S: You are demolishing your earlier statements, Callicles, and no longer searching adequately with me into the truth of the matter, if you speak contrary to what seems right to you.

C: And you do too, Socrates.

S: Then it is not right for me to do this either, if that is what in fact I do, or for you.

What does Callicles mean by "in order that my argument not become inconsistent should I say they are different, I will say they are the same"? Well, at 491e Callicles had recommended allowing one's "appetites to become as great as possible and not to hold them in check," and he did not place any restriction on what appetites were to be increased. Suppose that I have a raging appetite to scratch an itch, and I do so. I have experienced pleasure, the greater the pleasure the stronger my craving to scratch. Am I not therefore "living correctly" in accordance with the true Big Picture? Now suppose I have a raging appetite to live as a catamite, and I use my competence and courage and intelligence to do so without suffering any bad/painful consequences. Am I not therefore living pleasantly and therefore correctly and happily? Callicles's statement at 491e does implicitly identify pleasure (gratification of appetites) with the good and excellent life. Conversely, and by implication, a bad life would be a painful life. Pleasure is good, pain is bad. This is the entailment of Callicles's position at 491e, *and he recognizes this*.

So, he has one of two choices: (1) he can bite the bullet and accept the entailments of his position, that one can live happily and excellently by experiencing the strong pleasures of scratching or living as a catamite, *or* (2) he can deny that one is able to live a happy and excellent life simply by scratching or living as a catamite, but if he does this, he will have to introduce a distinction not made at 491e, namely, that the gratification of some but not all appetites is a good thing; some appetites, perhaps, should be allowed to grow great, but the gratification of some appetites is not good and one cannot live excellently by gratifying them, no matter how great is the pleasure of their gratification. At 495a Callicles adopts the first alternative, "I will say they [pleasure and good] are the same," counting on Socrates's inability to dislodge him from his position as long as he Callicles is willing to accept the logical consequences of it.

A person engaged in effective dialectic must be able to recognize what is and what is not entailed by a given position. If he is committed to position P he must be able to recognize what logically follows from P. Those logical consequences will fall into two classes—those he can accept and those he cannot. The former he need not worry about, at least initially; the latter, the unacceptable consequences of his position, pose a problem, for they possess the power to "demolish his earlier statements." If they are indeed consequences of his position P (and not merely apparent ones), and if he really cannot or chooses not to accept them, then he will need to introduce some modification of his original position P or surrender P entirely.

In the case before us, Socrates finally does succeed in bringing Callicles to recognize consequences of his position which he (Callicles) cannot accept: that good and excellent people *are no different* from bad and inferior people.[2] What then is Callicles to do? He must modify his original position. Far from its being the case that every pleasure is good and every pain is bad, there are in fact some pleasures that are bad and some pains that are good. The key distinction becomes not the one between pleasure and pain but the distinction between good pleasure (and good pain) versus bad pleasure (and bad pain), and this distinction is grounded on the distinction between the *beneficial* and the *harmful* (499d). Rather than its being the case that "good" is equated with pleasure and "bad" with pain, good should be equated with beneficial (pleasure *or* pain) and bad with harmful (pleasure *or* pain). And in order to distinguish the good pleasures/pains from the bad pleasures/pains one is going to need, what? One is going to need—knowledge! Expertise!

This book is not a logic text, and it would be off topic here to develop more examples of logical patterns of reasoning, however necessary familiarity with these patterns is for the effective dialectician. Let this summary suffice: since the truth about the Big Picture (if any truth about it does exist) will be gained by the exercise of reason, a person well qualified to search for and uncover that truth must possess expertise in the basics of logical argument and dialectic. These basics are not all that recondite or difficult to understand, but are none the less indispensable. If you are discussing with someone matters related to the Big Picture, it might help you to find out what that person knows about logic.

This exchange between Socrates and Callicles serves to high-

2. I omit consideration of Socrates's argument here, but it can be found at 497e–499b.

light a third trait of a good dialectician: *readiness to expect logical consistency from oneself and from others*. The basic patterns of logical argument are rules for maintaining consistency among the assertions one makes. To violate those patterns is to hold inconsistent positions, to fall into self-contradiction. There are various ways of expressing this law of noncontradiction. The way I learned it many years ago is that "a thing cannot both be and not be at the same time and in the same respect." For instance, the gratification of the same desire cannot be both good and not-good *at the same time and in the same respect*. Now it might be that the gratification of one desire is good and the gratification of another is not, or that the gratification of the same desire might be good at one time but not so at a different time, or that the gratification of the same desire at the same time might be good in one respect and bad in another. These statements do not violate the law of noncontradiction. But to assert that the gratification of the same desire is both good and not-good at the same time and in the same respect—that *is* to contradict oneself, and two contradictory statements cannot both be true because "a thing cannot both be and not be at the same time and in the same respect."

To tolerate logical self-contradiction in one's self or in others is to undermine the possibility of communication. Suppose I tell you that the gratification of the desire to scratch is good, but that it is also not good at the very same time and in the very same respect. What have I told you? Nothing: in fact, I have surrendered my ability to convey to you anything at all. Struck by my denial of the law of noncontradiction and just to test me, you ask me what time it is, and I respond that it's ten o'clock. Have I told you anything? No. Why not? You ask, could it also be not ten o'clock? No, I answer; the law of noncontradiction holds in this instance. Have I succeeded in telling you anything? No. Why not? Well, the law of noncontradiction holds here. You ask, does it also *not* hold here as well? Why can it not? I tell you it does hold and does not not-hold. And what does *this* statement mean? The law of noncontradiction does *not* not-hold, but why cannot it *also* not-hold as well? However I may try to answer, I am bound to fail to communicate anything to you. Once the law of noncontradiction is given up, even at a single point, the very possibility of communication collapses. Most people may not be aware of this, but the skilled dialectician is.

In addition to the first three traits of a good dialectician—the ability to ask the right questions, the ability to understand logical entailment, and the recognition of the importance of logical consistency, a fourth trait is also vital: the *ability to distinguish what is relevant to the topic and what is not*. This fourth trait, like the first and third, depends crucially upon the second. It is because I understand logical entailment that I am able to sort out remarks that are pertinent to the topic at hand from remarks that are not. Once one understands how dialectic operates and how the fundamental logical entailments work, the acquisition of the fourth trait is not particularly difficult. This is in marked contrast to the first trait, whose effective acquisition can take quite some time and may require a good deal of practice. But Rome was not built in a day, and no one promised that becoming a qualified searcher for the truth in ethics was going to happen overnight.

For the fourth trait, let us return to the beginning of the *Gorgias*. Of its four main characters we have seen all but Polus, a young man thrilled to have acquired the skill of oratory and eager to practice it at the drop of a hat. We have already been introduced to Callicles, but in the dialogue itself Polus serves as Socrates's principal interlocutor immediately after Gorgias. We recall that the dialogue opens with Gorgias, the professional teacher, coming to town and advertising his wares. But what skill is it that Gorgias promises to teach? The craft of oratory. Socrates induces his friend Chaerephon to ask, and what craft is that (448c–e)?

Polus: Many are the crafts among men discovered experientially from experience. Yes, indeed, it is experience which causes our times to march along in the way of craft, while inexperience causes them to march along the way of mere chance. For each of these crafts, some men take up one, others take up others otherwise, the best of men taking up the best. Gorgias here is of the best, and he partakes in the most admirable of crafts.

S: Admirably, O Gorgias, does Polus appear to have prepared himself for the giving of speeches, but what he promised Chaerephon, that he is not doing.

G: Just why, Socrates?

S: He seems to me to be answering the question not at all.... It is clear to me from what Polus has said that he has become practiced in what is called oratory rather than dialectic.

P: Why so, Socrates?

S: Because, Polus, with Chaerephon simply asking you for the craft about which Gorgias is knowledgeable, you shower it with praises as though someone were disparaging it, but as to what it is, that you have not answered.

P: Did I not answer that it was the most admirable?

S: Yes, indeed, though no one is asking what feature Gorgias's craft possesses, but rather what the craft is.

How shall I put this gently? Not everyone possesses Socrates's ability to distinguish what is to the point from what is not. Those who do possess it are frequently astonished to encounter others who appear fully satisfied, indeed enthralled, by (lengthy) discourse mostly or completely lacking in any content pertinent to the supposed topic. When I joined my present college more than thirty years ago, I was introduced to a pair of expressions that deeply impressed me. My new colleagues would say of someone that "so-and-so has (or does not have) a *per se* mind." Those who were thought to lack a *per se* mind were said to possess a *per accidens* one. People with *per se* minds are able to grasp the central point at issue and to detect what is germane to the truth about a topic and understand why it is germane. Those with *per accidens* minds lack or at least do not employ these abilities and so will say whatever may come into their head and may be satisfied or pleased with whatever comes into the head of anyone else.

To illustrate this distinction between *per se* and *per accidens* minds, let us look at a passage from the *Protagoras*, a dialogue which shares some obvious similarities with the *Gorgias*. The titles of both derive from prominent travelling teachers of virtue, known as sophists, who have come to Athens to offer their wares for sale. Protagoras, in fact, is an even more distinguished teacher than Gorgias, so his appearance in town cannot be anything but a cause for celebration. Hippocrates, a youthful acquaintance of Socrates, drags him out of bed while it is still dark, begging Socrates to accompany him to the house where Protagoras is staying. Hippocrates is clearly excited by the famous teacher of wisdom's arrival in town, but he is much afraid that he will be unable to overcome his own youth and inexperience when he speaks with the mighty Protagoras, and that the celebrated teacher will refuse Hippocrates's request to become one of the master's pupils. He therefore begs Socrates to come with him and plead on his behalf. Hippocrates's enthusiasm does not appear contagious, but Socrates nonetheless accedes to his request, and having waited until sunrise the two set out for Protagoras's lodgings. They find him surrounded by prominent Athenians delighted, as Hippocrates is, with the prospect of hearing speeches filled with the wisdom for which Protagoras is famous.

Protagoras claims to be a teacher of virtue, and since Socrates himself doubts whether virtue can be taught, he asks Protagoras to explain how virtue can be teachable (an exchange that recalls the *Meno*). Protagoras replies with a lengthy (320d–328d) oration, a "display."[3] Socrates says that he "kept gazing at him for a long time, simply enthralled, as though he were going to say more" (328d). Protagoras's speech had resolved all of Socrates's questions perfectly (328e–329b),

> except for one little stumbling block for me which it is clear Protagoras will easily explain because he has explained so many things already. If someone attended speeches on the same topic of any of the expert orators, he would probably hear words similar to this from Pericles or anyone else who was competent at speaking in public. But should he ask them something, like books they couldn't do anything, neither answer nor pose a question themselves. Should someone ask the least little point about something they have said, like bronze objects which have been struck they keep going for a long time unless someone grabs them. The orators are just like this. Being asked the littlest things, they keep on with their talk in the most wearisome manner. But Protagoras here, though capable of speaking beautifully and at length, as he has just now shown, can also if questioned answer briefly, and having raised a question can await the answer and deal with it—things which few are prepared to do. So now, Protagoras, I am in need of just one little thing, and I will have it all if you answer me this.

The "one little thing" that will lead Socrates to "have it all" relates to the apparent multiplicity of virtues: is virtue something one and unified so that to have one virtue is to have them all, or are the virtues differentiated and multiple and separate from one another, so that a person could possess one virtue without possessing the others? Protagoras responds by saying that "it is easy to answer you, Socrates" and that "virtue is one thing and what you are asking about [different virtues] are its parts" (329d). This answer by Protagoras, as you might surmise, raises further questions in Socrates's mind, and they are put in the form of the short give-and-take of

3. In the Greek "display" is a verbal adjective, and the underlying verb refers to the very same kind of activity we witnessed Polus undertaking in the passage from the *Gorgias* just quoted. Protagoras and Polus are both players in the game of "display."

question and answer, the process of dialectic with which the reader has now become familiar. The dialectical question-and-answer runs on for a considerable bit (329d–333e), or at least so it must have seemed to Protagoras, though it lasts only about half as long as the earlier speech which left Socrates positively "enthralled." Here is how the dialectical exchange winds (or unwinds) to its conclusion (333d–334a):

> S: Come now, starting again from the top, answer me this. Do some people seem to you to be prudent while they are acting unjustly?
>
> P: Possibly.
>
> S: And by "prudent" do you mean "to think ably"?
>
> P: Yes.
>
> S: And "to think ably" means "to deliberate well," that is, when they act unjustly?
>
> P: Possibly.
>
> S: Do they deliberate well committing injustice if it turns out well for them, or if badly?
>
> P: Only if it turns out well for them.
>
> S: Do you say that good things exist?
>
> P: I do.
>
> S: These things are good which are beneficial to people?
>
> P: Yes, by Zeus, and even if they are not beneficial to humans, I still call them good.
>
> S: (By this time Protagoras seemed to me to be feeling roughed up and flailing about and on the defensive against answering further. Seeing him in this condition, I cautiously adopted a softer approach.) Are you talking about, Protagoras, things that are of no benefit to any human being, or of no benefit whatsoever? Do you call *these* things good?

Socrates has just given a desperate Protagoras his way out, and Protagoras is not about to miss what may be his only chance of escape (334a–c):

P: Not at all, but I do know many things that are harmful to human beings, foods and drinks and drugs and a myriad others, and I know things that are beneficial; things that are neither beneficial nor harmful to humans but are to horses; things beneficial only to cattle or only to dogs; things that are beneficial to none of these but to trees, yes; things that are good for the roots of a tree, but bad for its buds, such as manure, good when spread around the roots of all plants, but if you wished to place it on shoots and new branches it will destroy them all. And then olive oil, very bad for all plants and most inimical to the hair of all animals except for the hair of human beings, and for this it is an aid, as it is for the rest of the body. And so the good is something complex and variable, such that this very thing, oil, is beneficial to a man for what's on the outside of the body, but the very worst for what is inside. And for this reason all doctors forbid sick people to use oil in the food they are about to eat, but only the smallest bit, only enough to suppress unpleasant smells in cooked foods.

And how does the audience receive this (334c–335a)?

S: (When he had spoken thus, the audience erupted into applause because he had spoken so beautifully! And then I said:) Protagoras, I sometimes happen to be a person of the forgetful type, and if someone speaks at length to me, I can forget what the speech was about. Just as if I happened to be hard of hearing and you wished to speak with me, you would think it necessary to speak louder to me than to others. So now that you have happened upon someone who is forgetful, chop up your answers for me and make them short if I am going to follow you.

P: How short are the answers you call on me to make? Shall I respond with answers shorter for you or shorter than necessary?

S: Not at all.

P: However long as necessary?

S: Certainly.

P: Then should my response to you be however long it seems to *me* necessary or however long it seems to *you*?

S: Well, I have heard that when you're teaching someone about these subjects, you are able to speak at great length, if you so wish, and never leave out a thing, or in turn to speak so concisely that no one ever spoke more concisely than you. So if you are going to speak with me, please use the latter style, concision.

But please, more about olive oil! Plato paints with rather vivid colors here, but he is making a key point: in order to be an effective searcher for the truth in any field, it is absolutely essential to be able to take what is said or written about a given topic and sift through it to find what is relevant to the truth while setting aside what is not. This takes a *per se* mind, and those who have one need to recognize that not everyone has such a mind.

In the process of bringing this chapter to a close, it will be of help to address a question that may already have occurred to the reader—why this focus on dialectic? Of course, dialectical situations do frequently arise in the context of debates, whether they be in formal settings, like political debates, or in informal contexts, like "bull sessions." But it would seem that in addition to these there are also many situations where reasoning is in play but there is nothing going on like the give-and-take of dialectical settings. A scientific researcher may be trying to figure out how to explain (or discount) an anomalous experimental outcome, or a writer may be composing a term paper or a book arguing some point of literary interpretation. In these last two situations something like research is being conducted, someone is trying to discover and argue for a truth about the topic of interest, but these are clearly not dialectic settings, are they?

Well, yes, they are dialectical settings, though we do not ordinarily think of them as such. The search for truth can be viewed as always *in some important respect* a collective effort. The common effort is easy to recognize when two or more persons explicitly participate in the endeavor, as we see in the Platonic dialogues. But suppose I am a scientific researcher or a writer of a book of literary interpretation; if I am *thinking* about the matter, trying to figure out the truth, I am reasoning about it, using patterns of logic to draw inferences to see what would follow from some assertion. And if I am doing that and doing it well, then I am also thinking about what might be said against some belief that I am tentatively considering as possibly true. And that means I am indeed engaged in a kind of dialectic, a dialectic or dialogue with myself as one putting forth an opposed point of view. Reasoning always requires at some level this give-and-take: "Okay, I think that I am right, but what might someone else say who disagrees with me and how might I respond in turn?" This is a putting of questions; not the questions that are addressed to us by another, but the questions we put to ourselves. Of course, if we are interested in a given topic, we may read up on it, and there we are likely to find several different and incompatible positions which have already been developed and reasons for each. There we already have a dialectical context, and we ourselves enter into it when we ask ourselves what we think about the different positions: do they hold water, how well can they answer objections that have been raised, can other objections be discovered, and can they be answered?

Our rational power, our ability to reason, is a power that is able to turn on and reflect upon itself. I work out an argument for some position, and then I reflect upon that argument to see if it is any good, if it makes its point, or if there is a mistake somewhere or an objection it cannot answer. The rational power is, in an important sense, never alone, never flying solo; if it is present, it is also present to look upon itself and the arguments it has produced and to examine them in precisely the same way another person could examine them. Every searcher for the truth is necessarily part of a company. The company may be formed by other people who are physically present or present merely by their words, whether found in print or transmitted in electronic media; or the researcher may be alone, but alone with himself and prepared to engage in a dialectical exchange with himself who, after all, may turn out to be his toughest critic.

The upshot: do not think of dialectic as something necessarily involving two or more people taking positions, asking questions of one another, and responding to others' objections. It may very well be that the best way to discover the truth is to work in collaboration with other people, but wherever there is thinking going on—inference-drawing, raising and answering questions, challenging answers—there is dialectic. The qualified researcher in any field of endeavor is a person skilled in dialectic.

Let us conclude this chapter by offering a summary and some reordering of the points made. In order to be a qualified researcher in the field of ethics, it is necessary that one possess the traits of a good dialectician. In this chapter we considered four of them. First, an understanding of the logical patterns of sound argument. This understanding goes beyond the mere ability to name the patterns of argument and to display them. It involves also a practical understanding of those patterns which is expressed in the ability to develop arguments for oneself in accord with those patterns *and* to detect the same patterns when they are employed in arguments developed by others.[4] Second, a readiness to demand logical consistency for the positions held by any given participant in the dia-

4. We saw three such patterns used in the *Gorgias*. (1) If the skill of oratory is said to be admirable because it can preserve your life safe and whole, *then it should follow logically* that the skills of swimming and engineering are also admirable because they are life-preserving, too. (2) If an excellent life is lived by allowing your appetites to grow as great as possible and then putting your competence to work to gratify those appetites, *then it should follow logically* that one could live an excellent and admirable life by gratifying the strong urge to scratch because gratifying your strong urge to scratch is an instance of allowing your appetites to grow and using your competence to gratify them. (3) If a position P which a person believes to be true has a logical implication X, and if the person is unable to accept the truth of X, *then it should follow logically* that the person should surrender his belief in the truth of P as it was originally stated.

logue, whether oneself or others. Consistency among assertions is determined by the logical patterns of argument, so that these first two traits are closely related.

Third, the ability to ask the right questions and to ask them in the right order. The purpose of asking questions is to test the soundness or truth of a position which has been asserted. If the position seems able to handle the questions raised, we have reason to believe the position is true. On the other hand, if the position seems to provide false answers to some of the questions, answers we cannot accept, the original position needs to be surrendered or at least modified in some way. This trait depends crucially upon, but is not limited to, possession of the first. Finally, the ability to distinguish what is relevant to the truth/falsity of a position from what is not relevant. Relevance is closely connected with the logical patterns of argument, so this trait also depends upon possession of the first.

Although these traits are in some respect "natural" to us whose nature is that of a rational animal, they need to be acquired and practiced. Courses and books in logic, dialectic, and rhetoric can develop and hone these abilities. Do-it-yourself manuals with titles like "How to Win Arguments" can be used to build on our natural abilities and improve them. Raw intelligence is important in this regard, but, as we shall see in part 3, the possession of high intelligence by no means guarantees that one will be good at reasoning. Raw intellectual ability is important but far from being the whole story.

7

DIALECTIC *and* ORDER

Getting Things Straight

Order (n.) "Formal disposition or array; regular, methodical, or harmonious arrangement in the position of the things contained in any space or area, or composing any group or body."

Hypothesis (n.) "A proposition or principle put forth or stated (without any reference to its correspondence with fact) merely as a basis for reasoning or argument, or as a premise from which to draw a conclusion; a supposition."

Vicarious (adj.) "Performed or achieved by means of another, or by one person, etc., on behalf of another."

In the previous chapter we considered four traits necessary for being a qualified researcher in any given area, and we used the phrase "good dialectician" to characterize such a person. A defense of those traits as being truly necessary for any qualified researcher in the field of ethics is reserved for the conclusion to part 2. In this chapter we will examine further traits necessary for a good dialectician. Some of them we have already come across in previous chapters, while others are new. After discussing these traits, we will have something more to say regarding the topic of misology which was raised in chapter 5.

The Ability to Recognize the Direction of Causal Order (*Euthyphro*)

The *Euthyphro*, you may recall from chapter 3, contains a discussion regarding the nature of piety and impiety. Socrates and Euthyphro chance upon one another on their way to court. On the one hand, Socrates has been charged, in effect, with impiety. Euthyphro, on the other, is prosecuting his father under highly ambiguous circumstances—a most dangerous act to perform, appearing as it does to run the risk of committing a serious act of impiety, *unless* Euthyphro were himself fully cognizant of the nature of piety and impiety. Since Euthyphro would not be so foolish as to act without such knowledge, Socrates believes he has found just the man who can help him with his case and so asks Euthyphro to explain precisely what piety is. Euthyphro complies (after some helpful prodding) with Socrates's request and answers that "what is dear to the gods is pious and what is not dear is impious" (7a).

The key thing to note about definitions is that they are the cause (the so-called formal cause) of a thing's being what it is. For instance, the definition of *man* is *rational animal*. A thing is a man (is a human being, a member of the species *Homo sapiens*) *because* the thing is a rational animal. It is *not* the case that a thing is a rational animal because it is a man. The definition of something refers to what is most fundamental in it and what explains and justifies the name of the thing's being correctly applied. For instance, the definition of "man" as "rational animal" justifies calling a particular individual a man when (and only when) that individual is a rational animal.

So, since Euthyphro defines "pious" as "what is dear to the gods," "what is dear to the gods" is fundamental to piety and accounts for and explains and causes some acts to be pious. This act is pious *because* it is loved by the gods. But see what happens in the following passage quoted above in chapter 3 (10d):

> S: What then do we say about the pious, Euthyphro? According to your account, is it not anything other than being loved by all the gods?
>
> E: Yes.
>
> S: Because it is pious or because of something else.
>
> E: No, it is because of this.
>
> S: So, it is loved because it is pious. But not: pious because it is loved.
>
> E: Apparently.
>
> S: On the other hand, because it is loved by the gods, it is therefore beloved and dear to the gods.
>
> E: Of course.
>
> S: So the dear-to-the-gods is not identical with the pious, Euthyphro, nor the pious identical with the dear-to-the-gods, as you maintain, but the one is different from the other.

What we see here is Socrates trying to point out to Euthyphro that the gods have reasons for loving the things they love, and that one of the reasons they have for loving something is that the thing is pious, a pious act. The gods love some actions by mortals *because* those actions are acts of piety. But *now* Euthyphro is brought to see that the causal relationship in fact runs in the opposite direction. What Socrates is trying to show is that in fact the move is from an act's being pious to its being loved by the gods, whereas Euthyphro recognizes that if his definition were correct, the move would be from an act's being loved by the gods to its being pious. The given act is *both* loved by the gods *and* pious; the question is, which is the correct order of priority, the order of causality?

In the previous chapter we noted the distinction between a *per se* and a *per accidens* mind. An individual with a *per se* mind will understand this point about the order of priority; a person without such a mind, possessing a *per accidens* mind, will find grasping this point a real challenge.

The Ability to Recognize the "Structure of Ordered Properties" in a Thing (*Through the Looking Glass* and *Sophistical Refutations*)

The first trait and the distinction between *per se* and *per accidens* minds are closely connected with the second trait. To explain and illustrate this trait, I have chosen two philosophers other than Plato—Aristotle and Charles L. Dodgson. The latter was a nineteenth-century philosopher of mathematics and logic who taught at Cambridge University in England. He published books on those topics, but he is best known for the books he wrote using the pen name Lewis Carroll. In the fifth chapter of *Through the Looking Glass*, Alice encounters the White Queen, who reports offhandedly that she possesses a memory which "works both ways." The dialogue picks up:

"I'm sure MINE only works one way," Alice remarked. "I can't remember things before they happen."

"It's a poor sort of memory that only works backwards," the Queen remarked.

"What sort of things do YOU remember best?" Alice ventured to ask.

"Oh, things that happened the week after next," the Queen replied in a careless tone. "For instance, now," she went on, sticking a large piece of plaster on her finger as she spoke, "there's the King's Messenger. He's in prison now, being punished; and the trial doesn't even begin till next Wednesday; and of course the crime comes last of all."

"Suppose he never commits the crime?" said Alice.

"That would be all the better, wouldn't it?" the Queen said, as she bound the plaster round her finger with a bit of ribbon.

Alice felt there was no denying THAT. "Of course it would be all the better," she said, "but it wouldn't be all the better his being punished."

"You're wrong THERE, at any rate," said the Queen: "were YOU ever punished?"

"Only for faults," said Alice.

"And you were all the better for it, I know!" the Queen said triumphantly.

"Yes, but then I HAD done the things I was punished for," said Alice, "that makes all the difference."

"But if you HADN'T done them," the Queen said, "that would have been better still; better, and better, and better!" Her voice went higher with each "better," till it got quite to a squeak at last.

Alice was just beginning to say "There's a mistake somewhere"—when the Queen began screaming so loud that she had to leave the sentence unfinished.[1]

Ah, but there *is* a mistake there somewhere, is there not? Look, you *are* better off for being punished, are you not? Of course you are. And you are better off for not having committed a crime than for having committed one, are you not? Of course you are. So if the King's Messenger is punished for a crime he ends up not committing, he is better off for being punished *and* for not having done it and Alice's worry is simply misplaced.

Well, something is indeed misplaced, but it is not Alice's worry. The White Queen has committed a common and important fallacy, the so-called fallacy of the accident. The fallacy consists in ignoring or getting scrambled the structure of ordered properties or the order of properties that a thing possesses. Let us grant to the White Queen that people are better off for being punished and that it is better *not* to have done something wrong than to have done it. But the *reason* why a person is better off for being punished is that he *has* performed the act for which he is punished and the benefit of punishment accrues to him as a means of correction or restoration for that wrong done. "Benefitted by being punished" is true of Alice *because* "committed a wrong" is *first* true of her.

Aristotle defined the fallacy of the accident in the following way (*Sophistical Refutations* 166b28–33):

1. *Alice's Adventures in Wonderland and Through the Looking Glass* (Oxford: Oxford University Press, 1998), 175–76.

> Fallacies arising from the accident occur when some feature [attribute, property] is thought to belong in a similar way to a thing and to its accident [any other true feature of the thing]. Because many features belong to the same thing, there is no necessity for *all* the features to belong to *all* the thing's predicates [true features] *and* to their subject [the thing itself] in a similar way. For example, if Coriscus is different from a man, he is different from himself, for he is a man.[2]

Aristotle's point is less difficult than it appears. Coriscus is a man, of course. And "man" is something different from "Coriscus." If this were not the case, then we who are men would all be Coriscus, and we are not. Now the fallacy of accident runs like this: since Coriscus is a man and man is something different from Coriscus, Coriscus is something different from Coriscus. No! The inference does not follow because the structure of ordered properties or the order of properties, in this case of Coriscus, has been ignored. "Different from Coriscus" *is* an attribute of "man," and "man" *is* an accident (attribute) of Coriscus but it does not follow that the true attribute ("different from Coriscus") of one of Coriscus's accidents ("man") is *also* a true attribute of Coriscus himself.

Properties are true of things in virtue of a precise order. "Better off for being punished" is true of Alice *only because* the property "committed some wrong" is *first* true of her. Remove the first property and the second property ceases to belong to her. Properties may be true of certain features or accidents of a thing without those same properties being true of the thing itself. A person with a *per se* mind recognizes that the properties of things stand in a particular order, and this order has at least two dimensions: (1) the order of *dependence and independence* and (2) the order of *transitivity and intransitivity*. "Better off for being punished" is true of Alice, but its being

2. *Aristotelis Topica et Sophistici Elenchi*, ed. W. D. Ross (Oxford: Oxford University Press, 1958); my translation.

true *depends* on another feature, that "committed a wrong" is *first* true of her. "Different from Coriscus" is true of "man" and "man" is true of Coriscus, but "different from Coriscus" is *intransitive* with respect to Coriscus himself.

A good dialectician, among other things a person with a *per se* mind, must understand the importance of grasping this ordered structure of properties. A person with a *per accidens* mind will have a hard time even making sense of this point and will encounter a further difficulty in appreciating its significance. To illustrate: imagine I were to ask you for an example of a "good pain," a pain that brings a benefit with it. The most frequent response to my request is the pain of exercise, a perfect illustration of the fallacy of accident. It is true that the act of exercising is beneficial and that it is painful, but it *does not* follow from this that the *pain itself* brings a benefit with it. To think that it does is to commit the fallacy of accident. True examples of "good pains" are the pains of a toothache or putting one's hand on a hot stove: *they* provide a benefit but *not* the pain of the beneficial action of exercising.

The Ability to Be Clear about the Point at Issue (*Meno*)

We saw this trait before in connection with our treatment of the *Meno* in chapter 2. Meno's opening question regarding the manner by which virtue is acquired leads Socrates in turn to ask what virtue is. If virtue were a form of knowledge, then we would expect that it could be taught, so that there would be teachers and pupils of it. But where to find teachers? Anytus rejects Socrates's first suggestion that the teachers of virtue are the sophists, travelling teachers who claim to be able to do just that. Where, then (92e–93b)?

A: But why is it necessary to mention the name of a particular individual? Any one of the Athenian gentlemen who he chances to meet will make him better than the sophists would, if he is only willing to follow that one's advice.

S: And did these gentlemen become such on their own, learning from no one but none the less being able to teach others, able to teach what they themselves have not learned?

A: I think they learned it from those who came before them, those who were themselves gentlemen, or does it not seem to you that there are many good men in this city?

S: Anytus, there do seem to me to be good men here who involve themselves in politics, and no fewer in the past. But this has been the point of our discussion—have the good men also been teachers of their own virtue—not whether there are good men here or not, and not whether there have been good men in the past. From the start we have been asking: is virtue teachable?

We saw above in chapter 2 that Anytus remains, simmering, believing that Socrates is "slandering our statesmen." But of course, Socrates is doing no such thing.

Recognition of the Importance of Definition (*Gorgias*)

We have seen this trait before, too, in our treatment of the *Gorgias* in chapter 1. Gorgias has come to town claiming to teach the craft of oratory. What is that, asks Socrates. Gorgias attempts an answer, but he succeeds only with great effort. At one point Socrates, sensing how bewildering all this must be to Gorgias, attempts to explain himself (453a–c):

S: Know well, Gorgias, at least so I have persuaded myself, that I am one of those who in a discussion with someone else want to gain knowledge of the discussion's subject, and I suppose you are one also.

G: So what, Socrates?

S: I will tell you now. About this persuasion produced by oratory—what you say it is and about what subjects—I want you to know that I do not have a clear understanding as yet. I do have a hunch about what you are saying and what oratory's persuasion is about; nevertheless, I will ask once again what you say this persuasion produced by oratory is, and about what subjects. And why, with my hunch, do I still ask and not speak for myself? It is not for your sake but for the discussion's sake, that it proceed so as to make what we are talking about absolutely clear to us.

The Ability to Recognize the Order in which a Discussion Should Proceed (*Gorgias*)

In our treatment of the *Gorgias* in chapter 6, we were introduced to the young and aspiring orator Polus, proud of his new career and proud to be associated with oratory, "the most admirable of crafts" (448c). Polus assumes Gorgias's role because he believes Socrates has dealt unfairly with Gorgias and he wishes to set the record straight regarding the wonderful craft of oratory. Socrates is pleased with Polus's offer to "set us upright" and get the discussion back on track, but he insists that Polus proceed not by way of "lengthy talk" (461cd) but by dialectical question-and-answer (462a–d):

S: If you have some concern about what has been said and wish to set it upright, as I was just now saying, modify whatever seems appropriate, taking part in questioning and being questioned, just as Gorgias and I did, refute and subject yourself to refutation....

P: Answer me, Socrates, since you think Gorgias has run into difficulties regarding oratory, what do you say it is?

S: Are you asking me what kind of *craft* [*technē*] I say it is?

P: Yes.

S: It seems to me to be no craft at all, Polus, if I am to answer you truthfully.

P: But what then do you think oratory is? ...

S: A kind of knack [*empeiria*].[3] ...

3. Another translation reads "routine." The word can also mean "experience," but two definitions of the cognate English word *empiric* suggest the point Socrates is trying to make here: (1) "one who,

P: A knack for what?

S: For producing a certain kind of gratification and pleasure.

P: Does oratory not then seem to you to be something admirable, being able to gratify people?

S: Really, Polus! Have you already learned from what I have said that you immediately ask me if I do not think oratory to be something admirable?

P: Have I not already learned that you say it is a knack?

But Socrates *must* think oratory to be something admirable, must he not (462d–463c)?

S: Would you like, since you value gratification, to gratify me just a bit?

P: Of course.

S: Ask me now what craft I think cookery is.

P: All right, I will. What craft is cookery?

S: Not one at all, Polus.

P: Then tell me what?

S: I say it is a kind of knack.

P: Tell me what kind?

S: I say, a knack producing gratification and pleasure, Polus.

P: So oratory and cookery are identical?

S: Not at all, but each is a part of the same endeavor.

P: What endeavor are you talking about? ...

S: There seems to me to be a practice that is not craft-like but for a mind capable of making accurate guesses,[4] bold and by nature clever at speaking with people, and I call the principal part of it fawning, flattery. There seem to me to be many other parts of this endeavor, one of which is cookery. This part looks like a craft, but according to my account it is not a craft but a knack and a routine. I call oratory a part of this, and cosmetics.... If then Polus wants to find out [the parts of flattery], let him find out, for he has not yet discovered what sort a part of flattery I claim oratory to be. But it has escaped him that I have not yet answered, and so he asks if I do not

either in medicine or in other branches of science, relies solely upon observation and experiment" and (2) "an untrained practitioner in physic or surgery; a quack."

4. Here Socrates alludes to the idea of "empiric" in both senses.

think oratory to be something admirable. And I will not answer whether I think it admirable or shameful before I first answer what it is. That would not be right, Polus.

Discussions must proceed in a definite order. The *first* task at hand is for Socrates to explain to Gorgias and Polus precisely what *he* thinks oratory is. Once that is achieved, *then* either of the others is free to rebut whatever Socrates has to say, but until Socrates has made this first point clear, the discussion of anything else is premature, pointless so far as the search for truth about oratory goes. Polus, on the other hand, thinks he has heard enough. All he needs to know is that Socrates believes oratory is a knack "for producing gratification and pleasure." And just what kind of pleasure and gratification is this? Socrates has not said because Polus has not given him the opportunity. When Socrates finally does succeed in making his own meaning clear, the phrase "knack for producing gratification and pleasure" takes on a strikingly different significance (464b–465a):

> S: I will show you more clearly what I'm saying, *if I can* [that is, if Polus here will let me].... Flattery is aware of [the parts of genuine craft-behavior] and (I do not say by *knowing* but by *clever guessing*) ... having put on the mask of each of the parts, presents itself as being that which the mask represents. It does not pay any attention to what is best [unlike all the crafts] but is ever at the service of the pleasant, and the *ignorant* person it seduces, so as to *appear* to be of the greatest worth.... I call this thing fawning flattery, and I assert that such a thing is *shameful*, Polus—yes, I am speaking this directly to you—because it shrewdly guesses at what is pleasant without paying attention to what is best. I do not call this thing a craft, but a knack and a routine, because it possesses no account for each of the instruments it employs, their nature in accordance with which it employs them, and so cannot state the cause of each thing, and I will *not* call so unreasonable a business a *craft*. If you disagree with these things, I am ready to engage in the argument.

A knack for producing pleasure and gratification. Something admirable? And what if it does not understand beyond this what it is doing and does not care, gives no thought to whether the pleasure and gratification is a good or is not a good? Still something admirable?

Polus's unwillingness, almost refusal, to follow things out in their proper order is a not uncommon trait. The good dialectician recognizes that however great may be the temptation to proceed in a way hostile to the achievement of full clarity and understanding, this temptation is ever to be resisted.

The Ability to Use Hypotheses Effectively (*Meno* and *Gorgias*)

We have seen this trait in our treatment of the *Meno* at the beginning of chapter 2. Meno's opening question—how is virtue acquired?—leads to Socrates's admission that he does not know what virtue is and has never met anyone who did. Not knowing what virtue is, how can Socrates hope to answer Meno's question? Well, he cannot hope to provide a fully satisfactory answer, but he is not stymied, not blocked from doing anything at all. Socrates begins by using examples from geometry, but he quickly shifts to the topic of virtue (87b–d):

> S: Since we do not know what virtue is or what it is like, let us examine it by working from a hypothesis as to whether or not it is teachable.... First, if it is something like or unlike knowledge, is it teachable or not? ... Is it not obvious to everyone that a person is not taught anything other than knowledge?[5]
>
> M: That seems right to me.

5. This last claim may be doubted, but two points noted in chapter 1 are relevant here. (1) Knowledge and belief are different things, and (2) by "teach" Socrates means "to impart knowledge."

S: But if virtue is a kind of knowledge, it would clearly then be teachable?

M: Certainly.

S: So we have quickly settled this issue: if it is of this sort [knowledge], it is teachable, if it is of that sort [not knowledge], it is not.

M: Clearly.

S: So given this, as it appears, we must examine whether virtue is knowledge or something other than knowledge.

M: That seems to me what we must examine next.[6]

The resort to hypotheses here is also an instance of the previous trait, for Socrates is proceeding in the proper order. Since he does not know the answer to the fundamental question, he *must* proceed by way of hypothesis. Two terms often used to mark such a dialectical move are *arguendo* and *ad argumentum*—"for the sake or purpose of carrying on the argument," for example, "let us suppose *arguendo* that virtue is a kind of knowledge." This logical or dialectical move gets us off dead center. We are not forced to argue off the bat whether virtue is a form of knowledge; rather, we can suppose that it is and see where that supposition leads us. If we do find people who seem to be able to teach virtue and people who seem to be able to learn virtue, we would at least have a start in answering the question of whether virtue is a form of knowledge. And if we do *not* discover such teachers and learners, well, that too is a help, suggesting that virtue is not a form of knowledge.

We have seen that dialectic is very much a process of question and answer, but it is also a process of testing hypotheses and plausible (or implausible) possibilities. The dialectician is able to start literally anywhere, from any suggestion that may have interesting implications. He may antecedently think he has good reason to believe that his supposition is in fact true, but he can also be in doubt

6. The passage from the *Meno* (87d–88c) quoted in chapter 2 picks up from here.

about it, or even be somewhat confident that the supposition is in fact false. Indeed, he can argue for the *falsity* of a position precisely by first assuming that the position is *true*, and then by showing that absurd consequences follow from that assumption.[7] We saw Socrates making this move in our treatment of the *Gorgias* in chapter 6.

So, Callicles, you think that a person can live an outstanding and excellent life by allowing his desires and appetites to grow as intense as they can become and then putting his ability at the service of gratifying them and in this way obtaining pleasure. Well, suppose that were true, Callicles. I, Socrates, do not believe that for a minute, but suppose you are right. Would it not follow in accordance with your own view that a person could live an excellent and happy and successful life by allowing his itches to grow great and then spending his life scratching those itches to his heart's content, scratching and scratching and scratching away? Yes?

At the close of the previous chapter we pointed out that whenever someone is thinking or arguing, he is always engaged in a dialectic exchange, even if it is only with himself. If I am working out some argument by myself, I am nonetheless always thinking about how someone else might object. It occurs to me that someone might say P. Well, what about that? What about P? Is it true? Let us look at it, see what might be said on its behalf. In doing this, I am assuming that P *might* be true; I am accepting P as a hypothesis, *arguendo*. The upshot: any person skilled in dialectic will recognize the importance of the use of hypotheses.

7. This is the so-called *reductio ad absurdum* form of argument.

The Possession of Relevant Knowledge and Expertise (*Laches* and Aristotle's *Nicomachean Ethics*)

We saw this trait at the opening of chapter 1, in the *Laches*: "So, we must first of all ask this very thing, whether any of us is an expert in what we are deliberating about, or not? If there is, then to obey him, even though he is only one, and forget the others. If there is not, then to search out someone else" (184e–185a). And in part 1 we developed the rationale for Socrates's insistence upon the possession of expertise by linking the following concepts together: (1) expertise/experience, (2) knowledge, (3) true belief tied down by an "account" or understanding of why the belief is true, (4) a roughly accurate picture or "map" of reality, and (5) the basis for successful action. We also suggested that the search for and the mere possession of knowledge might be good things in themselves, irrespective of whatever further advantage that search or possession might bring. The good dialectician will need, then, to know the relevant facts. The question remains: what *are* the relevant facts the good dialectician (the qualified researcher) *in the field of ethics* needs to possess. What is this information *about*?

The answer to this question is not far to seek: the qualified researcher in the field of ethics needs to possess knowledge of *human actions and their consequences*. After all, the primary search for ethics is the discovery of the best life I can possibly live: what does it look like and how should I begin living it? Aristotle draws an inference from this point in an early chapter of his *Nicomachean Ethics*: "A young person is not a competent hearer of lectures on political science [ethics], for he lacks experience of the actions that occur in life, but the discussions *start* from these and are *about* these" (1095a2–4).[8] Socrates himself (in the *Republic*) declares that the study of dialectic should not be assigned to students until they are about thirty years of age; he also insists that students be military veterans *and* well-trained mathematicians (537cd, 525a–528e). Without these traits, Socrates thought, students would be unlikely to benefit from their dialectical training.

Ethical discussions *start* from the "actions that occur in life" and are *about* these. Those adults familiar with the college scene often marvel how mistakes made by entering freshmen are identical to mistakes made by students who have preceded them. It is always the same story, and it is always the new freshmen who are taken unawares and surprised by the difficulties their actions bring upon themselves. Here is a simple rule to think about: *never be the first person to walk through a minefield*. (I hasten to add that I have great respect for bravery in military and nonmilitary contexts and that, for instance, a soldier who is ordered to clear a minefield is *not* a violator of this rule.) The point is: let the other guy (student) blow himself up. Just watch and see what happens to the other guy and then act knowing what happened to him. Actions that appear to have been successful perhaps should be imitated; actions that appear to have been damaging perhaps should not.

Although Aristotle holds that young people do not benefit from the study of ethics because they lack the necessary experience, the picture is really not quite that grim. As the previous paragraph suggests, it is possible for a young person to possess a significant amount of information about human actions and their consequences; although he has not had sufficient time to gain personal experience, it is always available to him to gain a significant amount of *vicarious* experience. *You* do not have to experiment with drugs to

8. *Aristotelis Ethica Nicomachea*, ed. J. Bywater (Oxford: Oxford University Press, 1894); my translation.

see what they are like; just see what happens to *other* people who use drugs—see how *their* lives work out and decide accordingly. The only way to gain first-hand personal experience of drugs is to use them yourself, but the vicarious experience available may suggest that drugs are one thing about which maybe you do not want to have first-hand experience.

Relevant information can be gained vicariously in many ways: movies, television, radio, books, magazines, journals, newspapers, the internet. Some knowledge of the fields of history, literature, psychology, and sociology is indispensable. One should strive to be abreast of empirical research, and some familiarity with the principles of statistics will be helpful. Of course, no one can hope to know everything, but the point is that a person is going to be a more effective dialectician to the extent that he possesses more empirical knowledge regarding facts and principles related to the topic in question.

Although sources of information and areas of study do provide a wealth of essential vicarious knowledge, there is (at least) one topic of knowledge which does require some first-hand personal experience—the knowledge of human foibles in oneself and others. People may be *rational* animals, but they are also rational *animals*, with all the emotionality that goes along with it: their emotional quirks, blind spots, attachments, stubbornness, and arrogance. Part 3 of this book is devoted to examining more carefully this last point; here we need only remark that the more one understands the idiosyncrasies and foibles to which human nature is subject, the better and more effective a dialectician he will be.

The Ability to Recognize the Level of Precision and Certitude a Particular Topic Permits (*Nicomachean Ethics*)

In the same chapter of the *Nicomachean Ethics* quoted above, Aristotle makes another important point (1094b19–27):

> We must be satisfied, when speaking of such subjects [those of ethics] and from such premises [as ethics provides], to point out the truth broadly and in outline, and in speaking about things which are true only for the most part and from premises of the same sort to reach conclusions of the same kind, and to receive in the same manner each of the things said. It is the feature of a well-educated person to seek precision for each kind of subject only so far as the nature of that subject permits. To accept plausible reasoning from a mathematician or to ask an orator for proofs are both evidence of poor education.

This is not an easy trait to acquire and probably requires extensive familiarity with the issues of a particular field, at least for those other than mathematics, but it is a particularly necessary trait for the qualified researcher in ethics. When has an issue been settled? When do we possess enough data to conclude we can be as certain about a particular question as we are ever going to be? And how certain can we ever expect to be about topics in a particular field? There simply is not one single standard of rationality and proof for all topics and in all areas. Mathematical fields possess rigorous and clear standards for rationality and acceptable proof; the empirical sciences not so much, though certainly there are clearer standards than those of the "human sciences," including ethics. But to say this is not to say that there are no standards of rationality and argument in the ethical sciences.

One possible reason for the disbelief in the existence of ethical knowledge, besides the one we have already highlighted in the opening "Apology," is the fact that arguments in ethics do not possess the same clarity and decisiveness as do arguments in the mathematical or even in the natural sciences. If you believe that there is only one standard for rationality and proof and that it is the standard of the mathematical or natural sciences, then you are going to conclude that ethical argument possesses little rationality. This inference may not be explicit in the minds of those who draw it, but it can remain nonetheless quite powerful with those who discount the possibility of ethical knowledge of any sort.

The expression "true enough to be worth saying" is particularly helpful. I take this expression to mean, "There is an important and useful truth here, but you'll be able to find plenty of exceptions to it." For instance, I mentioned that one should imitate actions that have been successful when others did them, avoid performing actions that were failures when others did them. I think that is an important and common-sense rule, but it cannot plausibly be construed as a rule to follow *always* and *everywhere*. There are just too many differences between people and their circumstances and their abilities to warrant making it a hard-and-fast guide to behavior. So, two things seem to be true: (1) irrationality can indeed arise precisely *because* people have disregarded the rule, and yet (2) a strict following of the rule is *also* a source of irrationality. Even though (2) is the case, the rule remains "true enough to be worth saying."

Ethics is about living the best life one can possibly live and becoming the very best person one can possibly become. Figuring out *how* to achieve this (much less *actually* achieving it) is no easy task, but it does not follow that it is also a hopeless, pointless task. Adopting the claim that there is no truth to be had about the Big Picture, that there are no true answers to the Really Big Question, has two important effects. It absolves me from the responsibility for trying to sift out the true from the false answers to the Really Big

Question, and for striving to conform my life as well as I can to the correct Big Picture. It also (for the reasons given in the conclusion to part 1) sinks my chances for discovering and living the best life, if there is one—and that is a shame, for I have only got one life to live.

I want to conclude this section with a suggestion; not an argument, but a suggestion. The suggestion is this: if one is trying to figure out what kind of acts are consistent or inconsistent with living the very best life possible, *a fundamental and central standard of rationality and rational action is what happens always or for the most part*. If the study of ethics begins with knowledge of human actions and their consequences, then this means that a fundamental and central standard of rationality and rational action is grounded upon knowledge of actions and their consequences that happen always or for the most part. A brief rationale for this suggestion will be offered in the next chapter.

The Ability to Recognize What Forms of Refutation Are "Worthless So Far as Truth Is Concerned" (*Gorgias*)

Although the *Gorgias* begins with a discussion of the nature and worth of oratory, what is of real interest to Socrates is (1) the connection between it and living a just life and (2) the question of the relationship between living a just life and living a happy life. Socrates himself is thoroughly convinced that the truly happy life is the just one, but he seeks anyone who might be able to point out whatever his mistake might be, if he has in fact made one. So, one acts well and happily when one acts justly, whereas acting unjustly is always to act miserably. Polus is astonished by Socrates's contention (470cd).

P: Oh so difficult to refute you, Socrates! Could not even a child refute you, showing that you are not saying what is true?

S: Then I would owe the child a great deal of thanks, and as much to you if you would refute me and relieve me of this foolishness. Do not grow weary doing good for a friend. Refute me!

P: But, Socrates, there is no need to mention ancient events in order to refute you. Things taking place right now are quite sufficient to refute you and show that many people acting unjustly are quite happy.

Polus cites as an example to prove his point the case of Archelaus, son of Perdiccas, then ruling as tyrant in Macedonia. The scuttlebutt, anyway, about Archelaus was that to reach the throne he had murdered his uncle, his cousin, and his half-brother. Polus continues: "And therefore, having committed the greatest injustices of anyone in Macedonia, he is the most wretched and miserable of all the Macedonians and not the happiest, and perhaps there might even be some Athenian, you to start with, who would prefer to be any Macedonian other than Archelaus" (471cd). Poor, *poor* Archelaus. Does your heart not bleed for him, miserable and wretched as he is, unjust as he is? It simply breaks your heart, does it not? The discussion continues (471d–472a):

S: At the beginning of our discussion, Polus, I praised you since you appeared to me as one well educated in rhetoric but to have neglected the practice of dialectic. And now is the argument nothing but this by which even a child could refute me, and have I now, as you believe, been refuted by you with this argument when I keep insisting that a person who acts unjustly is not happy? Where did you get that idea, my good man? In fact, I agree with absolutely nothing you have said!

P: You just do not want to say so, because you really do think it is the way I say.

S: You blessed man, you have undertaken to refute me in an oratorical manner, as people in law courts think that they are refuting: there, one side thinks it is refuting the other side when it brings forth many respected witnesses to what it has been saying, while the other side asserting the opposite offers only one witness or none. Such a "refutation" is completely worthless with regard to the truth; sometimes a person can be falsely testified against by many and well-respected people to be a certain sort. And now too, regarding the things you have been saying, just about everybody agrees with you, Athenians and strangers alike, should you wish to provide witnesses against me that I do not say what is true.

You have seen this style of "refutation" before, have you not? So-and-so *must* be wrong because everyone, or at least everyone among the respectable people, says he is.

Socrates does *not* mean here that every use of witnesses is illegitimate. No, what he is objecting to is the focus on mere assertions of "authorities" *instead* of the examination of the facts and arguments themselves. There are many occasions, of course, where we are not the experts and do not have access to the facts and arguments of those who are the experts in the field, and we are not in any position to familiarize ourselves with those facts and arguments. In these contexts, of course we must rely on the witness of expert opinion. What Socrates is thinking of here are situations where we could profitably look at the arguments and facts themselves and form our own conclusions (while also taking account of the opinions of others), but we rather choose to ignore those facts and arguments to focus instead just on the opinions of "respectable people" (who may or may not be genuine experts). It is this kind of "refutation" that is "completely worthless with regard to the truth." When it is possible, we should always insist on being shown the evidence and argument. Socrates continues (472bc):

But I, though only one, do not agree with you. You do not compel me, but bringing forth many false witnesses against me you undertake to banish me from my property, the truth.[9] And I, if I do not bring forth you yourself,

9. Socrates continues with his use of images taken from law courts.

though only one, as a witness agreeing with what I have said, I will think I have accomplished nothing worthy of mention concerning the things we have been discussing. And I think the same for you, if I do not testify on your side, though I am only one, and you leave all these other people aside.

The truth will be discovered not by the testimony of possibly ignorant and untrained witnesses, but by the dialectic conducted by people who possess and exercise the traits of the good dialectician (473b–e):

S: You think those committing injustice are happy as long as they do not pay the penalty.

P: Yes, indeed.

S: I, on the other hand, claim they are the most miserable and wretched, those paying the penalty less so. Would you like to refute this as well?

P: But this is even more "difficult" to refute than that other claim, Socrates!

S: Not difficult, surely, but impossible, Polus. What is true is never refuted.

P: What are you saying? A man is seized while doing an injustice, plotting a tyranny, and having been seized he is put on a rack, castrated, eyes burned out, and having been maltreated with many other great abuses of all kinds, beholding his children and wife mistreated as well, and at last he is crucified or covered in pitch.[10] And this man will be happier than if, having escaped capture he sets up as a tyrant and ruling in the city he lives out his life doing whatever he wishes, envied and thought happy by citizens and aliens. This you say is something impossible to refute?

S: This time you are scaring me, magnificent Polus, but you are not refuting. Just recently you were providing witnesses. Still, remind me again about one small point: whether the man plotting a tyranny was doing so unjustly, is that what you said?

P: Yes.

10. The word "crucified" here can also mean "impaled." Plato displays a fine touch here, does he not? Polus has the would-be tyrant viewing the maltreatment of his family after his eyes have been burned out.

S: Well, neither of them will ever be happier than the other, neither the one seizing the tyranny unjustly nor the one paying the appropriate penalty, for of two wretched people neither could be happier than the other. Still, the one who avoids getting caught and becomes a tyrant is the more wretched. What is this, Polus? You are laughing? Is this yet another form of refutation, to laugh when someone says something and not to refute?

Scaring and laughing at an opponent are as "worthless with regard to the truth" as the introduction of witnesses. The good dialectician, the qualified researcher in the field of ethics or in any other field, will recognize the methods of refutation to be worthless in the pursuit of truth. He will avoid using those methods in his own case, be able to point out when they are being used by others, and will not himself be swayed by their use, no matter how effective they may be in swaying the minds of others.

I will conclude this chapter by calling to mind a topic we encountered in chapter 5, "misology," the universal mistrust of reason, the idea that *no* argument is any good. If you remember, Socrates called misology something shameful because it arises in a person who is "without skill in reasoned argumentation," and when he is misled "blames neither himself nor his own lack of skill but ... shifts blame away from himself to the arguments" (*Phaedo* 90d). The cure for misology is acquiring the traits developed in this and the previous chapter. No one who possesses them will be a misologue.

8

GORGIAS, REPUBLIC, *and* THE ETHICS *of* *the* COSMOS

Cosmos (n.) "The world or universe as an ordered and harmonious system. Order, harmony, the opposite of *chaos*. [Greek *kosmos*—order, ornament, world, or universe, as stated by Pythagoras or his disciples, 'perfect order and arrangement.']"

When we left Polus and Socrates in the previous chapter, Socrates was maintaining that oratory was not a craft at all but simply a "knack" or "routine" for producing gratification and pleasure. It "presents itself" as something it is not, and proceeds by sheer "guessing" without in the least being able to provide an explanation "for each of the instruments it employs, their nature in accordance with which it employs them, and so cannot state the cause of each thing, and I will not call so unreasonable a business a craft" (465a). Far from being admirable, oratory in particular and knacks/routines in general are something "shameful" because they guess "at what is pleasant without paying attention to what is best" (465a). Genuine crafts, in contrast, always concentrate on the *good*, never focusing on whether the good brings with it temporary pleasure or pain. And just what is it that genuine crafts always aim at, this good which is only incidentally connected with pleasure and pain? In Socrates's discussion with Callicles, Socrates raises this vital question and supplies the answer—*order* (503d–504b):

> S: Let us consider how each craft keeps looking fixedly so that the object of its focus might take on definite features.... All the other craftsmen, each one looking toward its product, not selecting at random [its tools] does he apply them to his product, but in order that what he works upon may take on some shape. For example, if you would like, think of painters, house builders, ship builders, all the other craftsman, any one you wish, how each establishes each thing, whatever he establishes, for the sake of some structure, and forces one thing to be appropriate for and harmonized with another, until the whole object is put together as a work well structured and orderly. The other craftsmen and those we were just now mentioning, those concerned with the body, physical trainers and doctors, in some way provide order for the body and impose an organization on it. Do we agree that this is so, or not?
>
> C: Let it be so.
>
> S: So a house that comes to be organized and orderly would be good, one that comes to be disorganized would be in poor condition?
>
> C: I agree.
>
> S: Similarly for a boat?
>
> C: Yes.
>
> S: And we say the same for our bodies?
>
> C: Certainly.
>
> S: What about the soul? Will it be good if it comes to be disorganized, or organized and orderly?
>
> C: We must agree with this too, from what has been said.

We should not pass on without noting that Socrates's point is a universal one: if we think of *anything* we call good, it will be so because of the presence of a particular structure or organization in the thing's parts, and if we think of *anything* we call bad, it will be so because of the absence of this good organization and the presence of some kind of disorganization or lack of proper structure. (Socrates's point here seems applicable to manufactured objects and living bodies, but as we shall soon see, its scope is universal.) But his point raises a further question which is not answered or even hinted at in the *Gorgias*: what is it that makes a structure of a thing good and another structure bad? What is it that allows us to distinguish organization (good structure) from *dis*organization (bad structure)? This question will be examined in part 3.

Socrates's point appears unobjectionable. It is certainly plausible to think that whatever exists and has parts is good because of a particular kind of organization and bad because of a lack of that good organization. Fine, but is Socrates not moving too fast here when he assumes the existence of the soul? We have seen that same assumption at work before in chapter 5, where Socrates assumes he has a soul, and the only question for him is whether his soul will or will not survive its separation from the body. Why is Socrates so sure he has a soul in the first place? We ignored that question in chapter 5, but we can no longer avoid it and must now face it directly. We might agree that if the soul did indeed exist and have parts, then certainly, a good soul would be a soul with the proper organization and a bad soul would be lacking in that proper organization. But "who is to say" whether the soul in fact does exist? Maybe it does not, and then all this talk about the soul's survival and of good souls and bad souls would be completely mistaken.

The topic of the soul also arises in an early passage in the *Gorgias* (464a–465e) where the existence of the soul, like that of the body, is simply taken for granted by everyone. This seemingly gratuitous assumption is astonishing to contemporary minds, but that is because we fail to understand what the Greeks took to be the soul: *whatever* it is that causes a body to be alive. If everything in the world has a cause, then living bodies are caused to be living by something that exists and is, and Socrates and his Greek contemporaries called the thing that is and exists a "soul." Some bodies display evidence of moving on their own (or taking in nourishment or being aware of their environment), and others do not. The nature of this thing that causes some bodies to be living bodies rather than dead or inanimate (literally, "not animated" means "without soul") is a topic we need not address here. Maybe that thing is merely an arrangement of matter, maybe it is not. Maybe it will survive death, maybe it will not. All we need say here is this: if you have a living body, then you have a soul. Now this soul which you have may itself have many parts; and if it does, then your soul can possess a certain structure, and this structure might be properly organized (and your soul would be good) or not properly organized (and your soul would be bad).

We will worry about proper organization versus disorganization in part 3, but here we only need to look at what Socrates does with this universal principle of goodness (organization) as he applies it to the soul. Suppose your soul were a good one; it would therefore be properly organized, and your properly organized soul would presumably cause you to act "appropriately" (*Gorgias* 507ab). Socrates's assumption here is that *your soul can be and should be in control of and direct what your body does*, and it controls what the body does by *thinking*. (We will see Socrates's argument for this assumption in the next chapter.) One of the activities some living bodies perform but which nonliving bodies cannot perform is *thinking*. Thus, another piece of evidence we have for believing that there are things called souls is that some bodies engage in acts of thinking—they ask questions, disagree with interlocutors, etc. Nonliving bodies do not do that. So, if your soul is well organized and good, and your soul directs the actions of your body, then *presumably* the actions performed by your body but controlled by your soul will also be "appropriate." Because your soul is well organized, your actions controlled by your soul will themselves be well organized. Ah, yes, but what makes an action appropriate or well organized, an effect of a well-organized soul? Who is to say? In order to answer this question let us return to a remarkable statement by Callicles quoted above in chapter 6 (491e–492a):

> This is what is admirable and just by nature, what I say to you now with complete openness: the person who is going to live correctly must allow his own appetites to become as great as possible and not to hold them in check; and when they have become a great as possible, he must be competent to serve them with courage and intelligence and to fill them up whenever an appetite arises.

This statement illustrates nicely Callicles's conception of what a well-ordered, properly organized soul will look like, and how such a soul will act. If you are an excellent and outstanding human being, (1) you will cause yourself to have strong, raging appetites, but (2) you will also possess "courage and intelligence," and (3) you will use them to gratify those strong appetites competently, whatever their objects may be. In this way you will be leading an admirable and excellent life. Callicles elaborates on this ideal at considerable length. The naturally better and superior and stronger person will prey on the naturally worse and inferior and weaker person, using the weaker person for whatever gratifies the superior person's desires; and he thinks that self-control, the disciplining of one's desires and urges, is never for the naturally superior but only for "the stupid ones" (491e).

Unsurprisingly, Socrates has an entirely different idea. He expresses it in the following passage which I take to lie at the center of the *Gorgias*, at the center of ethics, indeed, at the center of human existence and life (507b–508a):

It is not a feature of a self-controlled person either to pursue or to avoid what is not appropriate but only as he should.... I set down these matters thus, and I assert them to be true. And if they are true, then someone wishing to be happy, so it seems, must pursue and practice self-control and flee licentiousness as each of us has the feet to do it ... not allowing his appetites to be undisciplined nor undertaking to fill them up, an endless evil, living the life of a brigand. Someone like that could be dear neither to another man nor to a god, for he could not be a partner, and wherever there is no partnership there is no friendship. Wise men say, Callicles, that partnership and friendship and self-control and things orderly and just hold together heaven and earth, gods and men, and because of this they call the whole of reality a cosmos, my friend, and not something disordered and uncontrolled. But you appear to me not to attend to these things, and though wise in these matters, it has escaped you that equality and geometry possess great power among both gods and men, but you believe that one should practice grasping for the greater share, and that is because you have neglected geometry.[1]

The universe to which Socrates points Callicles and us is a cosmos, an ordered system breathtaking in its magnificence. To appreciate this order and system is the highest exercise of the human intelligence, and to act in accordance with this order and system is to act as an excellent human being and to live the best possible life. It is an order which ties *everything* together—gods and humans, humans with one another in various forms of community, humans with the physical universe, humans with their natural environment, the parts of the body with one another, the parts of the soul with one another, the body with the soul. Ethics is a matter first of discerning that order "in which we live and move and have our being" and then acting in such a way as to preserve and extend that order. Ever against the effort of ethical action runs what I call the "law of moral entropy," a law which acts very much in the moral/ethical

1. Literally, "earth measurement," with the emphasis on *measurement*.

world as the law of entropy acts in the physical: I mean the constant tendency of all moral systems (the nonphysical systems) toward disorder and disorganization.

Callicles in contrast advocates a life of what turns out to be disorder, Socrates thinks, because he fails to grasp the order that surrounds him, the order in which he is immersed as a fish in water. And the reason Callicles fails to recognize and appreciate the order around him is that he has "neglected geometry." A reader may be tempted to see Socrates/Plato as not fully serious here. How could "neglect of geometry" possibly lead to the desperate, perhaps hopeless, condition of Callicles, even granting Socrates his entire point? Well, what is the study of geometry supposed to do? It is supposed to introduce us to an ordered and organized system which is (1) real, and (2) known only by the mind or intellect, and (3) to which the intellect must submit. The order in which we all swim as fish in water cannot be detected by the senses, but, at least according to Socrates, is as real and true as the order of geometry, and like the order of geometry, it is an order to which the intellect must submit if the intellect itself is to be properly ordered. A person who "neglects geometry" is a person who has failed to recognize and appreciate and submit to the most easily recognized (perhaps along with simple arithmetic) nonmaterial organized system there is; and having failed to recognize *that,* he will almost certainly fail to recognize and appreciate and submit to the other systems of order in which he is surrounded and submerged.

Callicles, as we saw above but did not put in these terms, does recognize one kind of order—the order of entailment among propositions. For instance, the two assertions (1) "the gratifying of any appetite in a competent manner is an instance of excellent and admirable living" and (2) "the urge to scratch is an appetite," are together closely ordered to (3) "the gratifying of the urge to scratch in a competent manner is an instance of excellent and admirable living." Callicles, then, is aware of the existence of at least some kinds of order, and in fact would have been aware of the order of geometry as well, but there are some orders about which he is oblivious. In part 3 we will consider a possible explanation for Callicles's blindness.

Before proceeding further we should ask the following question: *is* there in fact any such systematic interconnection of orders within orders? Fortunately, and perhaps not surprisingly, we need not argue for the actual existence of such order throughout. All we need to do here is to stipulate this as a possibility, and then note that the qualified searcher for the truth in ethics *must* be on the lookout to discern what systematic interconnections *might* exist and to grasp their implications. It would be irrational to assert the existence of such interconnections without any evidence or argument, but it would be equally irrational to deny their existence at the outset. Rather, at the beginning of any inquiry, the qualified researcher will be attuned to the possibility of systematic interconnections among aspects of the world which might at first sight seem unrelated. The researcher may or may not succeed in discovering any such interconnections, but he will not ignore their possibility and will be alert to discern them wherever they do exist. The good dialectician will always be on the lookout for these interconnections, since they could make a profound difference in the long run for living the best life possible, and the failure to observe them where they do exist could have devastating results. Callicles seems oblivious to the possibility of such systematic interconnection. Its non-existence appears to be an unconscious assumption on his part which underlies his ethical vision, and Callicles may in fact be right about this point. But note: Socrates is surely right too when he says that the life Callicles advocates is the life of a "brigand," and it is a life which does indeed make friendship and partnership and genuine sharing impossible.

The *Republic* arrives at the importance of recognizing systematic interconnection wherever it exists from an angle very different from that of the *Gorgias*. The *Republic* is about many things, but one of its most prominent topics is the nature of sound education, and a significant portion of the dialogue is devoted to a consideration of the process by which boys and young men (and girls and young women, for that matter) are educated to become capable rulers of themselves and their community. The capstone of this process is education in dialectic. Socrates notes two traits that all those who are to become competent in dialectic must have (537cd):

> The subjects they [the students of dialectic] learned as children *in no order* must be brought together for them into a synoptic vision of the kinship the subjects possess both with one another and with the nature of that which is [that is, reality].... The best test of the presence of a dialectical nature and its absence: the person capable of a synoptic vision is of a dialectical nature, the person who is not, not.... It will be necessary for you to be on the lookout for those who especially are of this sort ... testing them by the power of dialectic in order to discover who is able, while setting aside information from the eyes and other senses, to proceed with truth to *that which is* [in other words, to that reality which cannot be grasped by the senses but only by the mind or intellect].

Why, in addition to the first requirement of a synoptic vision, is there a second requirement of the ability to "set aside information from the eyes and other senses"? Because the orders within the cosmos are orders and systematic interrelationships which by their nature are not discernible by the senses. An illustration of this point will I think be of help here. Discussions of the morality of actions tend to focus on the individual agent and those persons directly and immediately affected by his actions. Take, for example, the topic of contraception. The act is thought by many to be justified because of its beneficial effects, all incurred by *particular* individuals—freedom from worry over unwanted pregnancy, avoidance of the consequences of unwanted pregnancy, pleasure for the agent and his or her partner, etc. What is there not to like?

Although the following observation may not be openly and explicitly acknowledged in many quarters, there nonetheless seem to be no grounds for disputing this claim: Europe at least appears to be going out of business. It appears that by the end of this century there could still exist countries *called* "France" and "Italy" and "Spain," but they will not be the *same* France or Spain or Italy that these countries were from their beginnings. You cannot have a Spain (or France or Italy) without enough Spaniards (or Frenchmen or Italians). And why will there not be enough Frenchmen or Italians or Spaniards? Because their birthrates are far below replacement level, so far below that there is (or at least seems to be) small chance of recovery. And why are their birthrates so low? Many reasons might be given for Europe's catastrophically low birthrate. Might a culture's acceptance of nonreproductive sexual acts, such as those using contraception, have a role to play in it? The good dialectician will be alert to the practice of asking such questions and keenly interested in their answers.

Socrates in the *Phaedo* offers a series of remarks which are pertinent here (65a–c):

> The philosopher especially, more than others, frees the soul from associations with the body.... It seems to most men that someone who has no experience of the pleasures that come from the body and has no share in them does not deserve to live and is almost drooping toward death.... Then what about the actual acquiring of knowledge? Is the body an impediment, or not, if someone in his search for truth brings along the body as a partner? I mean, for example, do sight and hearing provide any truth to hu-

mans, or are not even the poets ever telling us that we do not hear or see anything accurately, and surely if those two bodily senses are not precise or clear, the other senses must be less so, for they are all inferior to these? ... When does the soul attain to truth? ... Is it not in reasoning, if anywhere, that the truth of things becomes clear to it? ... And indeed the soul reasons best when nothing of such things disturbs it, neither hearing nor sight nor pain nor pleasure, but when it is most itself by itself, dismissing the body and as much as possible, not associating with it or being affected by it as it stretches out towards reality.

Systematic interconnections, if there are any, are not going to be detected through a focus on what the senses can reveal to us. But Socrates adds something else. The soul reasons best when "nothing of such things disturbs it, neither hearing nor sight *nor pain nor pleasure.*" This is a striking idea and well worth committing to memory. We will return to this passage in chapter 11.

Because the cosmos may be a close-knit web of systematic interconnections, five considerations should be kept constantly in mind. They are all interrelated, but their common theme of the importance of taking a broad view of possible interconnections warrants diverse emphases.

First, the expression "the road to hell is paved with good intentions." The belief alluded to is the assumption that because I *intend* my action or the policy I support to have consequence P and only consequence P, *therefore* my action or policy will *in fact* produce P and only P. It is interesting to note how commonly this mistaken assumption is made by individuals either regarding their own affairs or in organizational or political contexts. The good dialectician, experienced in the actions of life, knows that this assumption is all too frequently blatantly false. The world is far too complex for it to be true.

Second, the law of unintended consequences. This law is simply another way of making the same point: it is often foolish to assume that an action or policy will have only the good effects intended. In some instances this assumption may turn out to be true, but the knowledgeable and good dialectician will *never* have that law far from his mind.

Third, Murphy's Law, "what can go wrong will go wrong." The more complex a system, the more likely it is to "break," and the cosmos and many of its subsystems are extremely complicated. The practiced dialectician will not forget the import of Murphy's Law.

Fourth, the so-called Dionysian Principle. "Good results from a complete and integral cause, evil from a single defect." It is astonishing how routinely this principle is ignored, since it is of the utmost importance and immediately obvious to anyone when explained. To illustrate: what does it take to make a set of tires a *good* set of tires? Answer: *all* the tires have to be good. The set of tires is no better than its worst one. In order to make a good check of your tires before you go on a long road trip, you have to check *every* tire. Checking three of them is not enough. In order to perform a rationally adequate assessment of a system, *all* parts of the system need to be checked. Goodness (adequacy) is something that results from a "complete and integral and full" cause, evil (inadequacy) from even one single defect. Now of course there are degrees of adequacy and inadequacy, and a defect in a single part of a system need not be crucial in undermining the adequacy of the system as a whole. This is an imperfect world and we have to live with imperfections. That is why we build redundant systems. Nonetheless, the adequate assessment of any system requires attention to all parts of the system. The careful and skilled dialectician will understand the principle in its myriad applications.

Fifth, the difference between long-term versus short-term considerations. How important is this difference for the skilled dialectician? Answer: *nothing* could be more important. We believe this to be an absolutely necessary condition for growing in maturity, to be ready to think about not only the immediate, short-term consequences of an action but also the long-term, "strategic" ones as well.

In our presentation of the *Gorgias* in the previous chapter, we saw that Socrates had not actually bought into one of the assumptions upon which the dialogue up to that point had proceeded. It had been assumed from the outset that whatever oratory was, at least it was a kind or species of *craft*, and the dialectical search up until that point had been to find the features that served to mark off oratory from the other crafts. But upon Socrates's prodding Polus to ask him, Socrates revealed that he did not think oratory to be a craft at all but to be something shameful, a knack or routine for producing pleasure or gratification of the moment without attending in any way to the real good. Socrates continues: "So I say that cookery is the flattery that lies hidden under the guise of medicine. In the same way cosmetics lies concealed under the guise of gymnastics, mischievous, deceitful, ignoble, slavish, one that deceives by shapes and colors and smoothing and clothing, so as to present a loveliness not its own and to neglect the loveliness that is its own which comes by way of gymnastics" (465b). If Socrates is correct about this, how then is one to distinguish the reality from the appearance, the craft which aims at the real good from the knack which skillfully imitates craft but which really aims merely at flattery and pleasure and momentary gratification (465cd)?

They [the practitioners of the knack of oratory and another knack called "sophistry"] do not know how to make proper use of themselves, nor do others. Indeed, if the soul were not set in charge of the body, but the body were in charge of itself, and if cookery and medicine were not closely watched and distinguished by the soul but the body itself judged, measuring by the pleasures coming to it, then the world of Anaxagoras would very much be the case.[2] ... All things would be mixed up together in the same place, and things pertaining to medicine and health and things pertaining to cookery would be undistinguished from one another.

Why does Socrates refer to the distinction between body and soul here? And what does it mean that "the soul is in charge of the body" versus "the body is in charge of itself"? First of all, Socrates cannot mean to refer to a body separate from a soul because, as we have seen, such a body could not be alive. A clue to Socrates's meaning is found in the expression "the body itself judges, measuring by the pleasures coming to it." By "the body" here Socrates means to refer to the living body and its senses and to the soul which forms its judgments according to what the senses are telling it. Now the key thing about the bodily senses is that they are always about the present, the now. "My body" can tell me (my soul) how I am feeling now, whether I am *now* feeling good (pleasure) or bad (pain). "My body" in this sense *cannot* report about the future. It *cannot* tell me how I am going to feel in the next ten minutes or ten days or ten years. In order to acquire that information, I am forced to turn to something other than "my body"; I must turn to "my soul."

There are then two sources of information, "my body" which can give me information only about my present feelings, and "my soul" which can give me information (true or false) about how I will likely be feeling at some point in the future. When "the body is in charge of itself," the body (person) acts *solely* on the basis of how the body is feeling now. In contrast, when "the soul is in charge of the body," the body (person) acts on information not supplied to it by present sensations and feelings. Therefore, if the soul is not directing and governing the body but the body is directing and

2. A Greek philosopher (500–428 B.C.) who believed that the ordered and regular world we observe has emerged from a primordial chaos.

governing itself, the distinction between crafts and knacks collapses because no meaning attaches to "the good" as something distinct from "the pleasures coming to the body" which by their nature must be the *presently experienced or imagined pleasures*, and it is this very distinction upon which rests the distinction between crafts and knacks.

In our discussion of the importance of understanding logical entailments in chapter 6, we saw Callicles doing his level best to maintain in effect the superiority of the body's directing and governing itself, going so far as initially to concede the claim that one could lead an excellent and admirable life spending his time scratching to his heart's content. Ultimately, though, Callicles is forced to surrender his position and admit that some pleasures are good and others bad, the difference being between pleasures and pains that are beneficial and pleasures and pains that are harmful (499cd). Of course, the distinction between the beneficial and the harmful *cannot* be made by "the body," since all it knows is *present* pleasure and *present* pain, whereas the distinction between the beneficial and the harmful necessarily involves some reference to the future and is not confined simply to the now.

What happens if "the body is in charge of itself" and this distinction between the present and the future is simply ignored? Well, we might get lucky and nothing bad will happen, but the skilled and qualified dialectician will recognize that such a fortunate outcome should not be presumed. More often, as I am sure we have all experienced for ourselves, bad things can happen, though the bad things mostly happen in the *future* (518c–519a):

> S: Perhaps you would become angry if I were to say to you that you understand nothing about gymnastics. You are talking to me about servants, those who provide for the satisfaction of appetites, understanding nothing about what is good and admirable in these matters, and if it so happens,

filling up and fattening people's bodies, being praised by them even as they destroy their originally healthy flesh. The people in turn, because of their inexperience, will not blame their feeders as responsible for their illnesses and the dissolution of their originally healthy flesh but those who happen to be present at the time and offering them advice. But when that gluttony reaches them, bringing sickness with it much later, then because it is now shown to be unhealthy, they will blame and reproach and do something bad if they can to [the ones present and giving advice], and they will shower with praises those earlier people who are responsible for their ills. And you, Callicles, are now doing something exactly like that. You sing hymns in honor of [the famous Athenian statesmen of old] who feasted [the Athenian citizens of the past] and entertained them sumptuously with whatever they desired. [The Athenian citizens of the present] say that [the famous Athenian statesmen of old] have made the city great, but that the city is swollen and rotten underneath on account of those earlier statesmen, that they do not recognize. Without self-control and justice they stuffed the city full with harbors and dockyards and walls and tribute and similar foolishness. So when the fit of sickness comes, [the Athenian citizens of the present] will blame their advisors who are at hand and will shower praises on [the great statesmen of the past], those responsible for their evils.

The practiced and able dialectician will possess an acute awareness of the profound importance of thinking in the long term as well as the short term. This awareness must be joined with the second ability noted earlier in the quotation from the *Republic*, the ability to "set aside information from the eyes and other senses, to proceed with truth to that which is" (537d). The discernment of long-term consequences requires thought and reason. It is possible, and not uncommon, to approach matters of conduct by attending solely to "the body," to the particular and to the now, but when it comes to living the very best life possible, the good dialectician will recognize how vital it is for the "soul to be in charge of the body."

At the close of the discussion in the previous chapter, I offered a suggestion and promised a tentative explanation and defense. The suggestion was: "If one is trying to figure out what kind of acts are consistent or inconsistent with living the very best life possible, *a fundamental and central standard of rationality and rational action is what happens (or is true) always or for the most part.*" The tentative explanation and defense runs as follows.

First, the expression "what happens (or is true) always or for the most part" is intended to apply to the workings of nature generally but specifically to human actions and their consequences. Second, the suggestion that this provides "a fundamental standard of rationality and rational action" depends upon the truth of the wise person's claim mentioned in the *Gorgias*, "that partnership and friendship and self-control and things orderly and just hold together heaven and earth, gods and men, and because of this they call the whole of reality a cosmos, my friend, and not something disordered and uncontrolled" (507e–508a).

Suppose the universe is indeed a marvelously ordered, wonderfully interconnected cosmic system within which the human being finds himself. How then shall he best act if he is to live well? Presumably, he must live in harmony with that organized, deeply interrelated system of systems which is his home, to be in tune with that harmony, to preserve and protect and promote it to the best of his ability. Call it an ecology, but it is an ecology of cosmic proportions, and an ecology of political, familial, personal, mental, and bodily proportions as well. And how does one preserve and promote that ecology? Answer: by respecting it, which first requires the possession of a knowledge of it. And how does one go about acquiring knowledge of that ecology? Answer: by observing how the cosmos and all systems within it work. And how does the cosmos work? Answer: by regularities, by what always happens or happens for the most part. The idea I propose remains a suggestion. It could be argued for in a dialectical fashion, but I will not do so here, and the adoption of this suggestion will not be listed as one of the traits of the good dialectician. All we need to say is that the qualified researcher in ethics will strive to accord the suggestion whatever weight it deserves.

In order to be a qualified researcher in the field of ethics, it is necessary that one possess the traits of a good dialectician. In this chapter we considered three. First, the ability to focus on order and causal connections without being distracted by excessive attention to similarities and dissimilarities obvious to the senses. The senses of course do provide us with vital information regarding similarities and dissimilarities among the things in our world. But the rational order, the order of causal connection and dependence, is not apparent to the senses. Therefore, the good dialectician will not allow his thinking to be obscured by undue focus on what can be revealed to us merely by the senses. Second, a readiness to attend to the possibility of systematic interconnections among the features of the cosmos and an ability to note those interconnections where they exist. The good dialectician recognizes how important it can be to detect those interconnections wherever possible. Third, an appreciation of the importance of the so-called Dionysian Principle, that "good results from a single and integral (whole) cause, evil from a single defect." The good dialectician, in adopting the Dionysian Principle to guide his thinking, will be ever mindful of its applications, among which are the expression "the road to hell is paved with good intentions," the law of unintended consequences, Murphy's Law, and the importance of long-term as well as short-term consequences.

CONCLUSION *to* PART 2

Getting at the Whole Truth

Summarizing the conclusions of the previous three chapters, we can say that in order to be a qualified researcher in the field of ethics, the possession of each of the following traits is necessary:

(1) an understanding of the logical patterns of sound argument;
(2) a readiness to demand logical consistency for the positions held by any given participant in the dialogue, whether oneself or others;
(3) the ability to ask the right questions and to ask them in the right order;
(4) the ability to distinguish what is relevant to the truth/falsity of a position from what is not relevant;
(5) specific abilities in logic and dialectic, including the ability to:

recognize the direction of causal order;
recognize the "structure of ordered properties" in a thing;
be clear about the point at issue;
be clear about the meaning of the terms used in the discussion, recognizing the importance of definition;
recognize the order in which a discussion should proceed;

use hypotheses effectively;
recognize the level of precision and certitude that a particular topic permits;
recognize what forms of refutation are "worthless so far as truth is concerned";

(6) the possession of relevant knowledge, expertise;
(7) the ability to focus on order and causal connections without being distracted by excessive attention to similarities and dissimilarities obvious to the senses;
(8) a readiness to attend to the possibility of systematic interconnections among the features of the cosmos and an ability to note those interconnections where they exist;
(9) an appreciation of the importance of the so-called Dionysian Principle, that "good results from a single and integral (whole) cause, evil from a single defect," and its applications, among which are:

the expression "the road to hell is paved with good intentions";
the law of unintended consequences, that one should always be prepared to discern the possibility of consequences that are unintended but can nevertheless reasonably be expected to occur;
Murphy's Law, that what can go wrong will go wrong; and
the importance of long-term as well as short-term consequences.

In order to conclude part 2, I want to place once again before our minds the overarching context, stated in a passage from the conclusion to part 1. Is the lack of consensus regarding ethical issues a lack among qualified or unqualified researchers? And this question leads to two others: just what are the traits that make a researcher qualified? Further, is it question-begging to declare what those traits are?

The thrust of this book is to provide a resoundingly negative answer to the third question and to provide a list of such traits in response to the second. A person does not need to possess a proposed trait of a qualified researcher in ethics in order to recognize the proposed trait as indeed such a trait. This last assertion can only be supported by acting on it, and that is precisely what this conclusion sets out to do.

Remember the test: in order for a proposed trait to be included among the traits of a qualified researcher (the expression "qualified researcher" will be specified by the list of traits), it is necessary that everyone agree that the trait does indeed belong to any qualified researcher, and this "everyone" must include even those who lack the trait in question. In order to achieve what we set out to do, we need to put the traits uncovered in part 2 to the test.

In the first place, traits (1) through (5) simply express some of the essential features of logic, argument, and reasoning. Chapters 6 and 7 provide illustrations of each of them. They are the commonplaces of textbooks in logic and reasoning. How might someone object to them? Well, he could not do so by trying to use logic and argument, for these features simply *are* the canons of sound argument. If you are going to argue, you *must* accept features (1) through (5). Furthermore, those who believe there are *no* true and correct answers to the Really Big Question typically do have something like an argument for their belief, perhaps the one we developed in the "Apology": the argument from unresolved widespread disagreement, namely, since there is such disagreement, there is no truth about the Big Picture. But in order to make this argument, one must accept the canons of argument and therefore (1) through (5), which merely express those canons.

But now suppose someone responds, "I do not buy the practice of argumentation at all; it is just a fool's game, and I have no *argument* for that, I simply say that is the way it is. And not accepting argument at all, I do not have to buy into any of your canons (1)–(5)." And *that* is perfectly okay, too. So what? You do not have to accept the canons of argument; whether one does or does not accept the canons of argument is not and has never been the issue. The question is, always has been—what are the features of a qualified researcher in ethics? There may not be any truth about the Big Picture; and even if there were a truth, it might not be discoverable. But *if* there were a truth and *if it could* be discovered, what would it take to discover it? Well, it would take a lot of things, but one of the things it would take is *reason*.

Someone might reply, "No, it need not take reason at all; maybe it would just be through the senses or through some special insight or revelation." But the senses only give us knowledge of the present, and how would we *know* that this present experience is where excellence and truth and the admirable life lie *unless* one were to use reason? The same can be said regarding an appeal to some special insight or revelation. Furthermore, even if there is a truth to be discovered but it cannot be discovered by reason, *that cannot be known and should not be assumed in advance*. So, if there is a truth out there and it can be discovered, the qualified researcher is going to have to be equipped with the ability to reason, even if turns out that the truth is discovered in some other way. Therefore, traits (1) through (5) are necessary features of the qualified researcher in the field of ethics.

An analogous argument can be made for trait (6). What knowledge does the qualified researcher need to possess? Answer: whatever knowledge is necessary to discover the truth about the Big Picture. And what knowledge is that? We considered an answer to that question in connection with the discussion of that trait in chapter 7. Maybe other kinds of knowledge are necessary that differ from or supplement the ones mentioned in the earlier section? We will not suppose anything at the outset. The qualified researcher in the field of ethics will need to possess whatever knowledge is necessary or helpful in coming to the truth of the Big Picture; he will need to possess whatever expertise it takes. Trait (6), then, is a necessary trait of the qualified researcher.

An analogous argument can also be made for traits (7) through (9). There may in fact be no overarching, pervasive order in the universe to be discovered, or it may be undiscoverable. The senses may in fact not get in the way of the discovery of truth. The Dionysian Principle and its corollaries may not in fact be helpful in the discovery of the truth about the Big Picture. *But none of these possibilities can be known or should be assumed at the outset*. Traits (7) through (9) are therefore necessary features of the good dialectician, the qualified researcher in the field of ethics.

In the conclusion to part 1, we noted that part 2 would uncover cognitive or intellectual traits, while part 3 will deal with what may be called "moral" traits or features of desire. Having completed our search for the cognitive traits, we now turn to the "moral" traits. It is in part 3 that things really get interesting.

PART 3

ENSURING JUSTICE *in the* SOUL

9

REPUBLIC and the GOVERNOR

Govern (v.) "To direct or control (a person, the members of a household) with the authority of a superior."

Function (n.) "The special kind of activity proper to anything; the mode of action by which it fulfills its purpose."

Virtue (n.) "Superiority or excellence in respect either of nature or of operation; worth or efficacy of any kind. A particular power, efficacy, or good quality inherent in, or pertaining to, something."

In one of the examinations of the *Gorgias* in chapter 8, we saw Socrates identify a thing's goodness with its proper or best organization. Every craftsman aims at a good condition of the subject upon which he operates, and this good condition of the subject turns out always to be a good kind of organization of the parts of the thing he operates upon. In connection with Socrates's point, we raised two questions: (1) how does one determine what the best organization of any given thing is? And (2) what would it be for a soul to be in a well-organized or a badly organized state? To answer the second question, we have to raise another: (3) what are the parts or aspects of the soul that might be well or badly organized? We will begin by uncovering the aspects of the soul and then see what would make a soul good or bad (well organized or badly organized). In the process of answering the second and third questions, we will develop a *universal principle* that will provide an answer to the first. Following up on the examination of the soul in this chapter, we will turn to a consideration of the principal forms of disorganization in the soul in chapter 10. We will conclude part 3 with a completion of our search for the traits of a good dialectician in chapter 11.

Upon first reading, many people take the *Republic* to be a political dialogue. And it certainly is that, but political matters are secondary to Plato's principal focus, the soul (368de, 592ab). Plato is first of all interested in uncovering and displaying the nature of the human soul so that we might arrive at a true understanding of where goodness and badness in the soul (and by extension, successful and failed living) precisely lie. And if goodness depends on order and best organization, and order and organization depend on a thing's having "parts," then Plato's first question has to be: what are the "parts" of the soul, and how do we go about discovering them?

If the soul is that by which we are alive, then it is to our experience in living we must look if we are to discover the parts of the thing by which we are alive. We must appeal to our own experience. And what does our experience tell us? First, we encounter situations in which we note *internal opposition or conflict*. Plato's fundamental assumption here is that if we experience opposition within ourselves, there must be at least two "things" within us capable of opposing one another (439a–e):

> S: The soul of the thirsty person, insofar as it thirsts, wishes for nothing else than to drink, and strives for this and is eager for this.
>
> Glaucon: Clearly.
>
> S: Then if anything draws it back while it is thirsting, there is something in the soul different from that which thirsts and drives it, like an animal, to drink. For we say that the same thing with the same part of itself

concerning the very same thing cannot act in such opposite ways.[1] ... Shall we say that some people although thirsting refuse to drink? ... What, then, should one say about them? Is there not within their soul something calling upon them to drink, and something forbidding, the thing controlling being something different from the thing calling for drink? ... So it is not unreasonable that we believe these are two things and different from one another, naming that by which the soul reckons its rational feature, and that by which it loves, hungers, thirsts, and is agitated by other desires its irrational and appetitive feature, a companion of various satisfactions and pleasures.... Let these two forms within the soul then be taken as having been distinguished by us.

Does the soul then have only these two parts, the rational and the appetitive (439e–440c)?

S: But now what of the spirited feature by which we become angry, is it a third or is it of the same nature as one of the others?

G: Perhaps it is like one of the others, the appetitive.

S: I once heard something which I believe, that Leontius son of Aglaion, going up from the Piraeus on the outside of the northern wall, and becoming aware of dead bodies lying beside the place of public execution, simultaneously desired to see them *and* was vexed with himself and turned away and for a time struggled and covered his eyes, but finally overcome by his desires and opening his eyes wide he rushed up to the dead bodies and cried out, "Behold for yourselves, you wretched things, and be filled with such a lovely sight." ... Surely this story illustrates the point that anger sometimes does battle against desires as one thing against something else.... And in other circumstances do we not frequently notice that when desires assault someone against his reason he reviles himself and is angered with that which assaults him from within, and as though two factions, the spirit of such a person becomes an ally of the reason? ... And

1. The *Republic* is the second longest of Plato's works and contains lengthy passages without any of the dialectical give-and-take we have been accustomed to see in other dialogues, though the dialogue form is nonetheless retained. For brevity, then, I have omitted most of Glaucon's responses, those which are only *pro forma*. Other passages from the *Republic* of a similar nature will also be shortened in this way.

what about this? When someone believes himself to have acted unjustly, is it not true that the nobler he is the less is he able to become angry even though he is hungry or freezing or suffering in some other way from the person whom he thinks to be acting justly in doing these things to him, and as I say his spirit refuses to be stirred up against such a one?

Socrates's principle that "the same thing never does or undergoes opposites according to the same respect toward the same thing" (436b) and our own personal experience together yield the conclusion that our soul contains at least *three* separate "parts": that by which we think and reason, that by which we get angry, that by which we desire and crave (436a). Having arrived at these parts, we can say that the good soul is a soul in which the three parts—the rational, the high-spirited, and the appetitive—are properly ordered and organized with respect to one another. Yes, but on what basis then can we claim that the parts of the soul are properly and best organized? In order to answer this question we need to examine two concepts which we will find to be of profound importance (352d–353c):

S: Does there seem to you to be a work or function of a horse? ... Would you acknowledge that the work or function of a horse or of anything else is what someone does with it alone or with it best?

Thrasymachus: I do not understand.

S: Consider this. Could you see with anything other than eyes? ... Could you hear with anything other than ears? ... Do we not rightly claim that these are the functions of those things? ... You could cut the branch of a vine with a dagger or a carving knife or many other instruments ... but with nothing, I think, as well as with a pruning knife made for this.... Shall we not set this as its function? ... I think you have now better understood what I was just now asking, trying to find out if this is not the work or function of each thing, whatever it alone does or does better than anything else.... And further, does there not seem to you to be a virtue or excellence that belongs to each thing as well as its function for which it has been fashioned? Let us go over the same ground again. We say there is some function of the eyes? ... And so there is a virtue of the eyes? ... And some function of the ears? ... And so a virtue? ... And what about *all* other things? Is it not the *same*? ... Could the eyes ever perform their function well if they didn't possess their distinctive excellence but instead possessed their distinctive evil or defect opposite to their excellence?

Thrasymachus: How could that be? I take you to be speaking of blindness rather than sight.

Socrates is working toward the statement of a universal principle (353cd):

> S: Whatever their excellence is. I have not asked about that, but only whether it is by its own particular excellence that a thing performs its own function well, doing whatever it does, and by its own defect does badly.... And the ears deprived of their own virtue will perform their function badly.... And do we then accept the *same* reasoning for *all* things?

The *same* reasoning is said to apply to *all* things, but not really to all things, but only to things that have a function. Some things in the world do not, at least as far as we can tell, possess any function at all: pebbles or sticks, for example, though a function can be *assigned* to them—we might use a few pebbles to scatter birds which are eating from our garden, or use a stick to give us a rough measure of something's dimensions. But other things in the world possess functions that are not *assigned* to them. Some of these are artificial and have been *designed* by humans to perform a function and serve a purpose; their function is not *assigned to* them but *designed into* them. On the other hand, some things in the world seem to possess functions entirely independent of any design or assignment on our part. There are certain natural bodies that at least give the appearance of having been designed by someone to perform a function and serve a purpose—sight for the eyes, hearing of the ears, etc. The function is the distinctive activity or "work" of a thing. Socrates's rough-and-ready test: what only this thing can do, or what this thing can do better than any other thing, *that* is the function of the thing.

Where we have function, then, we have activity, and activities can be performed well or badly. Take two hammers. Hammer 1 performs its function well, it hammers well; we call it a good hammer. Hammer 2, on the other hand, performs its function badly, it hammers badly; we call it a bad hammer. Now why is this? Clearly, there must be some difference between Hammer 1 and Hammer 2 that accounts for the fact that Hammer 1 hammers well and Hammer 2 hammers badly.

Remember what we have already learned about the aim of every craft from our treatment of the *Gorgias* in chapter 8: every craft always aims to make the subject upon which it acts as good as possible, and it does so by producing the best organization possible in that subject. If Hammer 1 is a good hammer, then it must be properly organized (from the *Gorgias*); and it is a good hammer because it is good at performing its function, that of hammering well (from the *Republic*). In contrast, Hammer 2 is a bad hammer and therefore badly organized; but it is a bad hammer because it performs its function badly. So there it is: good versus bad organization is determined by the function of a given thing. In order to judge whether something is good or bad, the craftsman must be able to detect whether it is well or badly organized; and in order to do *that*, he must be able to recognize whether it performs its function well or badly; and in order to do *that*, he must understand the thing's function in the first place. It is the thing's *function* which is fundamental to a thing's proper organization and therefore to its goodness.

Here is the universal principle alluded to above: for anything with a function, it is good because it possesses the proper organization or structure that enables it to perform its function well. In contrast, anything with a function will be bad when it cannot perform its function at all or can do so only badly, and this will be because the thing lacks its proper ordering or structure. Fair enough, but does the soul possess a function? In chapter 8 we suggested what that function might be, but in the *Republic* Socrates argues for it (353de):

> S: Is there some work of the soul which you could perform with absolutely nothing else in the world, such as this: to be in charge of, to rule, to offer counsel, and all such things? Is there anything else than to the soul we might rightly assign these things and assert these to be its distinctive work? ... What about life? Shall we not assert this to be unique to the soul? ... And do we not also assert there to be an excellence or virtue of the soul? ... Will the soul ever perform its own work well if deprived of its distinctive virtue, or is that impossible?
>
> T: Impossible.
>
> S: So necessarily it belongs to a bad soul to rule and govern things badly, and to a good soul to do all these things well.

First, the function of the soul is to govern. We introduced the idea of the soul's being in charge of the body in chapter 8 as something required for the ability to recognize the distinction between crafts and knacks mentioned in the *Gorgias* (465cd):

> If the soul were not set in charge of the body, but the body were in charge of itself, and if cookery and medicine were not closely watched and distinguished by the soul but the body itself judged, measuring by the pleasures coming to it, then the world of Anaxagoras would very much be the case ... all things would be mixed up together in the same place, and things pertaining to medicine and health and things pertaining to cookery would be undistinguished from one another.

We also saw earlier that when Socrates refers to "the body," he cannot be referring to the body as distinct and separated from "the soul," because such a body could not be a living body, and Socrates here is thinking of a body which is alive and can "judge" matters pertaining to cookery and medicine. Rather, by "the body" in this context Socrates means the living body with its senses and its ability to judge whether it is *now* experiencing pleasure or pain.

Why again is it the function of "the soul" (its thinking but not sensing part) to be in charge of "the body" (the living body with its senses and its ability to feel pleasure and pain)? Remember Socrates's test: the function of a thing is what only it can do or what it can do best. Now, can the body govern the soul? That is, can a person's senses and pleasures and pains direct what he does and how he thinks? Certainly, but things often do not work out very well when this happens, do they? So the body *can* govern the soul but that would not be the body's function if the body's governance is not *the best*. The body, remember, only knows the present; it is only the soul which can be aware of future events, the long-term consequences of what the body does. Things *can* turn out well when the body governs, and things *can* turn out badly when the soul governs, but the question is: which is the *better* governor, *by nature*? Governing will be the function not of whatever *can* govern but only of whatever can govern *best*. If the soul is a more effective governor than the body because of its being able to know long-term consequences, then it is the function of the soul to rule.

The two passages quoted from the *Republic* (352d–353c and 353cd) also contain the extremely important idea of a thing's "excellence" or "virtue." A thing will be able to perform its function well when it possesses its own excellence or virtue, whereas it will be impossible for it to accomplish its own work well if it lacks that virtue. What does this mean? Well, let us go back to our example of Hammer 1 and Hammer 2. Hammer 1 is able to perform its function well, it hammers well, because it possesses its own excellence and virtue, whereas Hammer 2 is incapable of accomplishing its work well because it lacks its virtue. What does Hammer 1 have that Hammer 2 lacks? Good and proper organization, as we have seen. And what is that? Here we can say, the possession of the "excellence and virtue" of their own, the excellence and virtue of *hammers*.

A virtue of hammers is simply the "good quality inherent in or pertaining to" hammers, a feature which is a "power or efficacy" in hammers, a feature which makes hammers efficacious, effective (good) at being hammers. Hammer 1 is a good hammer because it can be used to hammer well, and this is because it possesses the proper organization for hammers. This proper organization of hammers is nothing other than the presence of the *complete* set of features that are the powers and efficacies of hammers, the features that make hammers powerful, effective at hammering things, at performing their function well. On the other hand, the deprivation of *one* or more of those features makes for bad hammers, for hammers incapable of functioning well as hammers. Opposed to *virtues*, which are sources of power and efficacy in a thing, are *vices*, which are therefore sources of weakness and inefficacy in the thing, features that hinder the thing from performing its function well, or even from performing its function at all.

Here is the full version of the universal principle stated above: *for anything with a function, it is good because it possesses the proper organization or structure which enables it to perform its function well, and this proper organization is the presence of all its virtues and absence of all its vices*. In contrast, anything with a function will be bad when it cannot perform its function at all or can do so only badly, and this will be because the thing lacks its proper ordering or structure. This lack is identical to the absence of one or more of the thing's virtues and the presence of one or more of the thing's vices.

I have devoted a considerable amount of attention to the presentation of this principle because of its importance in connection with the idea that the soul has a function: governing the body. We can sum up by saying that (1) the soul will be a good soul because it is able to perform its function well, that of governing the body; (2) it will be able to perform its function well because it has its best and proper organization; and (3) it will have its best and proper organization because it possesses *all* of its virtues and excellences and *none* of its vices and defects. Goodness depends on best organization, best organization depends on the presence of virtues, and virtues depend on function. There are as many virtues of a thing as there are features necessary for the thing to perform its function well.

Given the three parts or aspects of the soul, and given the soul's function, we can now determine what the best organization of the soul must be if it is to perform its function well, and also what the soul's distinctive virtues are (*Republic* 441e–442d):

> Does it not belong to the rational part to rule, being wise and possessing forethought for the benefit of the entire soul, and to the spirit to be subject and to battle on its behalf? ... And these two ... will be set over the appetitive which is the largest part of the soul in each person and by nature the most insatiable for wealth. This part is to be carefully watched lest by being stuffed with what are called the pleasures of the body and becoming extremely strong, it does not perform its own proper work but undertakes to enslave and rule the other parts, a thing which does not belong to it by nature, and overturns the life of the whole soul?[2] ... Would not the other two be especially good at guarding against enemies from outside for the sake of the entire soul and also that of the body, one counseling, the other battling and following the ruling part and by its courage executing what had been counseled? ... Brave I think we call each person in virtue of this part in him when his spirit preserves while experiencing pains and pleasures what has been handed down by the reasoning part concerning what is to be feared, what not.... Wise by that tiny part which ruled in him and handed down these things, holding firm within itself the knowledge of what is beneficial for each and for the whole community of these three beings.... And is the person not self-controlled by the friendship and harmony of these same things when the ruling part and the two ruled parts agree that the rational part should rule and the others not rise in rebellion against it?

2. Note that this is the perfect response to Callicles (*Gorgias* 491e–492a).

If the soul is a natural entity with a natural function of governing the body, we should not be surprised to find that each of its natural parts has its own function. The function of governance belongs to the rational part in virtue of its "possessing forethought for the benefit of the entire soul." It is because the rational part can form some estimate of the future that it has the right to rule and is therefore "superior" by nature to the other parts. In order to exercise well its function of governance by taking forethought, it will need the virtue of *wisdom*, the feature by which the rational part knows what in fact will be best for the person as a whole. The spirited part has the function of "battling" while "following the ruling part." It is the part by which we face difficult and dangerous situations for the sake of the good of the whole person, and so it will need the virtue of *courage* in order to perform *its* function well. But in doing so, it must "follow the ruling part" and act in accordance with the rational part's directions, lest it face danger in a way that is foolish or unnecessary or otherwise harmful to the well-being of the whole person. Finally, Socrates does not mention explicitly here the function of the appetitive part, but its function is that of pursuing objects that are in some way helpful or necessary for the person's survival and well-being, things pleasant to the senses like food and drink or things useful to the person like wealth and possessions generally. To do this well, the appetitive part will need the virtue of *self-control* by which it pursues those objects but not excessively and contrary to the judgment of the rational part.

If the rational part possesses the virtue of *wisdom*, the spirited part the virtue of *courage* or bravery, the appetitive part the virtue of *self-control* (also called "moderation" or "temperance"), then the soul will display "the friendship and harmony of these same things when the ruling part and the two ruled parts agree that the rational should rule and the others not rise in rebellion against it." When there is harmony and friendship among the different parts, then the spirited and appetitive parts will not act as "brigands" in bringing about the destruction of the beauty and order and harmony and cosmos of the soul in relation to its surroundings.

We thus have three of the four so-called cardinal (from the Latin *cardo*, "hinge") virtues, but where is the fourth, where is *justice*? "We surely have not forgotten this, that a city [*polis*] is just by each of the three classes in it performing its own function.... We need to remember, then, that each of us will be just whenever each of the parts in him performs its own work, the person himself attending to his own affairs" (441de). Such a person, as we saw in the *Gorgias*, will act appropriately toward the gods and other humans and the *cosmos* at large, but in the *Republic* Socrates explains in more detail what the source of these appropriate acts is: "The cause is that each of the things within him performs its own work with respect to ruling and being ruled" (443b). In contrast, the commission of injustice arises from a more fundamental disorder in the soul, "a kind of sedition of these three things, an interfering and meddling and uprising of one part against the whole of the soul" (444b). Socrates draws the distinction between justice and injustice in the soul by likening them to health and disease in the body (444c–e):

> Justice and injustice turn out to be no different from healthy and unhealthy things, these for the body, those for the soul.... Healthy things produce health, and unhealthy things disease.... Then performing just actions produces justice and unjust acts injustice? ... But to produce health is to establish the things in the body *according to nature* with respect to ruling and being ruled by one another, whereas to produce disease is to establish the things in the body *contrary to nature* with respect to ruling and being ruled by one another.... And so, is it not the case that to produce justice in the soul is to establish the things in the soul *according to nature* with respect to ruling and being ruled by one another, whereas to produce injustice is to establish the things in the soul *contrary to nature* with respect to ruling and

being ruled by one another? . . . Virtue then, as it seems, would be a kind of health and beauty and good condition of the soul, and vice would be a disease and ugliness and weakness.

Just actions are order-preserving and order-promoting because they *arise from a more fundamental and prior order* in the soul of the doer of just actions. On the other hand, unjust actions destroy order and produce disorder in people's lives and in the cosmos because they proceed from a deeper *disorder already existing in the soul* of the wrongdoer. Doing right is its own reward, wrongdoing its own punishment, for the former contributes to a healthier, stronger, more beautiful soul, whereas the latter contributes to making a soul weaker, uglier, and more diseased.

Socrates draws this point forcefully in the *Gorgias*, picking up on an idea we covered in chapter 6, that if staying alive were the main goal that an excellent person should have, then the crafts of swimming, piloting ships, and engineering would themselves be admirable and worthy of great respect, since they are clearly important for promoting the goal of an excellent life: survival. But with regard to the ship's pilot, Socrates observes (511e–512b):

He disembarks and walks along the seaside and ship with a modest demeanor. I suppose he has reflected and knows that it is by no means clear which of his fellow voyagers he has benefitted by not allowing them to drown in the sea, and which he has harmed, knowing well that they are no better when they disembarked than when they embarked, either in body or in soul. He considers that if someone afflicted with serious and incurable diseases in the body did not drown, such a person is wretched for not having died and has received no benefit at all from him. But if someone has many incurable diseases in what is more valuable than his body, his soul, his life is not worth living for him, and the ship's pilot does not help him if he rescues him from the sea or prison or any place else. And he knows that for a corrupt person it is better not to be alive, for he *necessarily* lives badly. For this reason it is not the practice for the pilot to cover himself with glory even though he keeps us alive, nor for the engineer either, my marvelous fellow [Callicles].

According to Socrates, the goal of a truly excellent person is this (507c–e, 512e):

> Someone wishing to be happy, so it seems, must pursue and practice self-control and flee licentiousness as each of us has the feet to do it, and especially must make sure to be in need of no punishment.... This appears to me to be the target by which, looking to it, one must live, stretching out toward this with all his resources and those of the city, that justice and self-control will be present in one preparing to be blessed.... To live whatever length of life is allowed as a true man rather than as a clinger-to-life ... and concentrate on one thing only, the manner by which he might live the remaining part of his life in as excellent a way as possible.

A few points to make for the sake of accuracy, and then the conclusion of this chapter. In the account quoted from the *Republic*, Socrates assigns wisdom exclusively to the rational part, bravery exclusively to the spirited part, but does not assign any virtue exclusively to the appetitive part. Moderation or agreement about who is to rule is a virtue shared by all three of the parts. In the philosophical tradition stemming from Plato it became customary to assign moderation or self-control exclusively to the appetitive part, and doing so does make things a bit neater—one part, one unique virtue. Something analogous, though a bit more complicated, happened to the virtue of justice. Further developments also led to divisions within the rational and the appetitive parts. Fortunately, none of these complications need concern us, since we will have plenty on our hands as it is.

So there we have it, justice and injustice. The former a kind of health, strength, beauty, harmony, cosmos; the latter a kind of disease, weakness, ugliness, disharmony, chaos. The former is virtue; its possession allows "the soul" (the rational part) to govern effectively "the body" (the bodily parts of the soul and the living body itself). The latter is vice; its presence hinders or renders impossible effective governance by the rational part. When that happens, chaos results. Plato noted four principal forms of injustice. His characterization of them contains some of the most striking commentary he ever wrote, and its acuteness has never been surpassed. To those four principal forms of injustice we now turn.

10

REPUBLIC and the FOUR FORMS *of* INJUSTICE

Character (n.) "The sum of the moral and mental qualities which distinguish an individual. Moral qualities strongly developed or strikingly displayed. [Greek charaktēr, instrument for marking or graving, impress, stamp, distinctive mark, distinctive nature.]"

Moral (adj.) "Of or pertaining to character or disposition, considered as good or bad, virtuous or vicious; of or pertaining to the distinction between right and wrong, or good and evil, in relation to actions, volitions, or character of responsible beings; ethical."

Tyrannical (adj.) "Of the nature or character of a tyrant; acting or operating in an oppressive, cruel, or unjustly severe manner. Of, pertaining to, or befitting a tyrant; severely oppressive; despotically harsh or cruel."

In the previous chapter we examined Plato's treatment of the soul and its parts or aspects, and what a good, well-organized soul would look like, what virtues it would have. In this chapter we will look at his conception of bad souls—souls that lack proper organization, disordered and diseased souls, souls in a condition of vice. If the main features of justice are harmony, beauty, strength, and health, then the souls we will be examining in this chapter are instances of disharmony, ugliness, weakness, and disease. Plato believes there are four principal types of diseased souls, what we will call conditions of "psychic disease" in contrast to somatic disease. Psychic disease and mental illness are not identical—one can be mentally ill without being afflicted with any of the conditions mentioned in this chapter, and one may be subject to psychic disease without suffering mental illness—although, as we shall see, psychic disease can easily bring on mental illness and mental illness may display many of the symptoms of the conditions discussed here. Disentangling psychic disease and mental illness in a particular clinical case may be nearly impossible. Why Plato believes there are four principal kinds of psychic disease will become clear as the chapter develops.

Before examining the individual types, we would do well to have before our eyes one of the most famous images in the *Republic*, what Socrates calls "an icon of the soul in words" and what he believes will help us see more clearly the respective natures of justice and the four types of injustice (588c–e):

> Form, then, a single shape of a manifold and many-headed beast, having the heads of tame and wild animals roundabout in a circle, able to change them and cause to spring forth from itself all such heads.... And then another shape, one of a lion, and then one of a man, and let the first be far the largest and the second be second in size.... Then form together these three into one, so that they in some way grow together.... And then form around them on the outside the image of one, that of the man, so that to the person unable to see inside but able to see only the external covering it appears to be one living thing, the man.

From what we have already learned regarding the three parts of the soul, it should not be hard for us to recognize these same parts in their new representations—the rational part as the man, the spirited part as the lion, and the appetitive part as the manifold and many-headed beast. The relative size of the three parts in this "icon in words" is intended to suggest the relative inherent strength of the soul's three parts. The small size of the man within suggests the difficulty reason encounters in imposing its rule over the appetitive and spirited elements.

We have already seen that justice in the soul (beauty, strength, harmony, health) occurs when there is "unanimity" about which part is to rule—the rational part, due to its power of "forethought" and its possession of the virtue of wisdom. We will see that each of the four types of injustice lacks this subjection by the nonrational to the rational, though in different ways. One of the four types is the condition of a soul whose "lion" (spirited) part is in control; two of the four are those of a soul whose "many-headed beast" (appetitive) part is in control; and the last type of injustice, the worst, is that of a soul subject to a particularly terrible form of psychic disintegration and disorder. All of this we shall see shortly.

The four types of injustice and the condition of justice can all be understood as types of *character*, so before going any further it will help if we have before us an understanding of what character is. From the definition given at the beginning of the chapter we can see that a person's character may be understood as "[the set of] moral qualities strongly developed or strikingly displayed" by the person. By "moral qualities" we mean features that are at least somewhat under a person's control and bear on his being able to live the best life he can possibly live, whether for good or ill. Such qualities will be "strikingly displayed" in one of three ways: (1) with regard to *thought*, the beliefs a person is inclined to have regarding topics related to the best kind of life possible; (2) with regard to *action*, the actions a person is inclined to perform or avoid performing; (3) with regard to *emotions*, the feelings a person is inclined to have about certain situations, actions, and persons. Note that all three features are given in terms of inclinations or dispositions to think, act, and feel in typical or characteristic ways. So with regard to character, we are more focused on what a person is inclined or predisposed to do (or think or feel) than on what he in fact is doing (or thinking or feeling) at any given moment. Since one's character is a disposition to act and think and feel, it is in an important sense deeper within than the actions we happen to be performing or the beliefs and emotions we happen to have at any particular time. Dispositional traits of character are sometimes called "second nature," because when acting from character we act from a deep part of ourselves and so act with ease, elegance, and effectiveness. Acting against character will always be difficult. It is also worth recalling in this context a quotation from the English poet Ben Jonson (1572–1637): "Language most shows a man, speak that I may see thee."[1] Your stated opinions say much about *you*.

Plato's treatment in the *Republic* of the four types of injustice weaves together considerations of two sorts, societal/political and individual. We can speak about the character not only of an individual but also of an entire society or culture. How does this work? Well, in the first place, if a sufficiently large number of individuals in a society possess a particular character, this will have an effect on the overall tone of a society or culture in the form of a set of *social expectations* regarding the sorts of actions, beliefs, and feelings a person should possess and display, versus those he should not. Also, culture, by its expectations, is a powerful formative source of the characters of individuals within it by encouraging them to think, act, and feel in a particular way. Influential people within a culture serve as role models, and others pattern their actions, beliefs, and

1. *Timber: Or Discoveries Made upon Men and Matter* (New York: Barnes and Noble, 1966), 78.

emotions on the lives of the famous ones they observe. We turn now to the four characters of weakness and ugliness.

"Timocratic" Character— Control by the "Lion"

"Timocratic" derives from two Greek words, one for "honor" and one for "control." It's the character where the honor-loving, spirited part of the soul is in control of the person's life, and this control is "strongly developed and strikingly displayed." What follows is a summary of Plato's characterization of a timocratic person, symptoms of the particular form of disorder that is distinctive of the timocratic character.

Because the spirited element is predominant, one feature of the timocratic character stands out: the importance of being "number one." Fame, status, and power are the goods which make up the excellent life. Noteworthy regarding the timocratic person is his competitiveness and ambition for advancement. Life is a zero-sum game; the world divides into winners and losers. This character may display itself as being obstinate in argument because argument is viewed as a contest, and any acknowledgment of error becomes an admission of defeat. Plato also mentions a fondness for sports and hunting. Obviously, the point here (and for the other characters as well) is not that these features are bad in and of themselves, this desire to win and make something of oneself, but that it is possible to have too much of a good thing. The injustice and disorganization of this condition consists in that fact that one centers one's life on the pursuit of goals which simply do not merit such all-consuming preoccupation. The rational part is not in control because the goods of the timocratic ideal are *not* goods which the rational part, independent of influence from the irrational, would affirm as the supreme goods about which the best life is appropriately centered.

The rational part of the timocratic person does not see the error of his ways because the rational part has been subjected to control by the "lion," the spirited part. And why is this? Because the *emotions* of the "lion" have gotten out of hand. They have become too strong and thus have blurred or distorted or blinded the vision of the rational part. And how did this happen, how did the emotion of the "lion" get out of hand? A number of suggestions might be offered, and Plato provides one—the presence of an excessive amount of the emotion of shame, a deep sense of inferiority, and a corresponding need to assure himself of his own worth (449e). Deep down, the person of timocratic character suspects he may very well be a loser, and so experiences the need to prove himself good and worthwhile by showing himself to be better than others as a winner over them. A feature of the timocratic character that bears special mention is an acute sensitivity to someone's place in the hierarchy of things, an excessive submissiveness to the higher-ups coupled with harshness toward those of lower status or lower in the chain of command. Both private enterprise and service in the public sector attract timocratic characters, encouraging in them a perhaps already overdeveloped willingness to do whatever it takes to get ahead, to get to the top, to achieve the prize, to win (548c–550b).

"Oligarchic" Character— Control by the "Many-Headed Beast"

"Oligarchic" also derives from two Greek words, the word for "control" and the word for "few," so the term literally means "rule by the few," but since the rich are always relatively few in number, the term came to mean "rule by the (few) rich." The "many-headed beast," it turns out, possesses two different kinds of desires—the desire for stuff, money, wealth, "gain" in general, and the desire for sensual pleasure. In the oligarchic character it is the first desire that controls the person. What follows are a few symptoms of the disorder that is the oligarchic character.

Since the oligarchic person identifies the chief good with wealth (possessions generally), wealth is the measure of excellence and intelligence. People who are not rich tend to have an inferior status in the eyes of oligarchic characters. These characters are often thrifty and hardworking hoarders. They lead an ascetic existence while trying to turn a profit in every situation. They are concerned about their reputation, but will commit criminal acts whenever there is "ample power for committing injustice," such as the guardianships of orphans (554c). Finding it difficult to spend money in the pursuit of other goals, the oligarchic character "fights in the oligarchic manner employing few of his resources and is usually defeated, but he remains rich" (555a).

Plato suggests that the source of an oligarchic character may lie in feelings of insecurity or a sense of vulnerability. The world is a dangerous place, and wealth and possessions generally are necessary to protect oneself from external threats and accidents (553a–555a). As with the timocratic character, the rational part of the oligarchic character is controlled by the nonrational, in this case desire for the good of "stuff," a good not worthy of the central importance assigned to it by the oligarchic person. Emotions lying in the "many-headed beast" have become so strong as to distort the rational part's vision of the real good. It is worth remarking that some people who strive for riches are not true oligarchs. They desire their wealth only as the "trophy" and proof of victory in some competitive arena. As this point shows, people can display some mixture of two or more characters.

"Democratic" Character—Control by the "Many-Headed Beast"

Like the first two terms, "democratic" also derives from two Greek words, one for "control" and one for "people." It is important to divest this term of its inevitable political connotations. The *demos* is the mass of ordinary citizens, however they may be inclined to vote. Like the oligarchic character, the democratic character is one in which the "many-headed beast" is in control, the difference between them being the kind of good paramount in the mind of the person with that character, wealth versus pleasure. Plato devotes considerable space to detailing the features of the democratic character, and his description is particularly impressive.

Since the democratic character sets pleasure as the supreme good, all other goods will be viewed as instrumental to it. Plato suggests that this character arises from some form of deprivation. He subscribes to a principle which might be called the law of moral opposition: "Excessive action in one direction is likely to produce in turn a change toward the opposite direction, and this occurs in seasons and in plants and in bodies and not least in political communities" (563e–564a)—and, I would add, in characters.

Plato highlights two features of the democratic culture and character which serve as bulwarks protecting the pursuit of pleasure—equality and freedom. All pleasures must be treated as equal, and freedom is essential lest the pursuit of pleasure be impeded.[2] To suggest that not all pleasures are equal, that some are superior to others, is anathema to the democratic culture and character. The

2. From our treatment of Callicles in the early part of chapter 6 (particularly 491e–492a,c), we can see that Callicles is a perfect specimen of the democratic character.

single, unforgivable sin is that of holding and expressing the view that some pleasures are inferior to others, that some lifestyles are worse than others. Plato notes of democratic characters that whenever "some restriction of any kind is introduced, they are vexed and refuse to bear it.... They wind up paying attention to none of the laws, written or unwritten, so that in no way shall anyone be ruler over them" (563de).

"Tyrannical" Character— The "Law of Moral Entropy" at Work

The word "tyrant" originally meant a ruler who had taken absolute control of a government contrary to law and without the right to do so.[3] A tyrant may have ruled in a gentle and just manner, and a few of the tyrants of the ancient Greek world did just that; but many of the tyrants did rule in an oppressive, corrupt, and cruel fashion, and the word soon took on the connotations it now has of cruelty and oppression.

The tyrannical character is not defined through rule of the soul by any particular element but rather through the *manner* in which that rule is exercised. Plato's conception of the tyrannical character is what has come to be called the "addictive personality." A person of democratic character, "having assigned his pleasures equal status, lives ever handing over the rule of himself to whichever desire happens to present itself, as if selected by lot, until it is satisfied, and then to another, dishonoring none but nurturing them equally" (561b).[4] But to nurture a desire is to grow the desire. And a de-

3. Examination of the tyrannical character is not necessary for the purposes of part 3, but it has been included for the sake of completeness and for its interest and general usefulness.

4. Plato continues using language taken from politics—many of the offices in a democracy were filled by lot. His point is that the person's devotion to his particular passion is by chance, lacking any rational justification.

sire once nurtured may subside for a time but it can return with renewed vigor. Nurture enough desires over a long enough period of time, and the odds are that sooner or later one of them will wrench control from the person, turning him into a "drunken, lustful maniac," now at the mercy of some "particular lust," some desire for power or pleasure or possessions.

Thus, the tyrannical character is not defined by a conception of the good different from those of the timocratic, oligarchic, and democratic characters. Rather, this character differs from the others by the degree to which the false vision of the good controls the soul. In the first three characters, the rational part is placed at the service of the pursuit of the distinctive and defining good of that particular character. To act intelligently is conceived as effectively pursuing honor or wealth or pleasure, but in such a way that the overall well being of the person is not obviously damaged. In the tyrannical character this semi-autonomy of reason—or better, its apparent autonomy—is lost, the rational part is demoted even from its servant status, and the person becomes totally enslaved to the "particular lust." A person of tyrannical character now pursues the particular good in a manner that no longer carries even the semblance of control by the rational part. The difference, shall we say, is like that between a heavy drinker and a raging alcoholic.

Because of the tyrannical character's enslavement to his "particular lust," he is unstable and therefore incapable of genuine friendship. Promises mean nothing—they will be kept only if they do not collide with the dictates of lust. "He is envious, untrustworthy, unjust, without friends ... bad luck to himself, and then makes those around him like himself" (580a). In contemporary terminology, the tyrannical character is dysfunctional and disordered, spreading disorder, creating enablers and co-dependents around him (572e–580a).

What we see at work here is what in chapter 8 was called the law of moral entropy. States of character and societies have an inherent tendency to "wind down," to become increasingly disorganized. Characters and cultures will seek the democratic level much as water flows downhill, because the democratic culture is the most attractive of all cultures owing to its variety and the welter of goods, characters, and "lifestyles" to be found in it—freedom, equality, and pleasure, or in the immortal words of Callicles, "luxury and licentiousness and liberty."

But recognize that the unwinding of character and culture does not end there. Remember what we said earlier about the law of moral opposition. A more extensive quote will be helpful (563d–564a):

> [The citizens of democratic cultures] wind up paying attention to none of the laws, written or unwritten, so that in no way shall anyone be ruler over them.... This is the beginning, so lovely and vigorous, from which tyranny sprouts.... The disease that arising in oligarchy destroyed it, the same disease arising in democracy, but more widely diffused and stronger because of freedom, enslaves it utterly. In truth, excessive action in one direction is likely to produce in turn a change toward the opposite direction, and this occurs in seasons and in plants and in bodies and not least in political communities .... Excess of freedom is likely to change itself into nothing else than excessive slavery, both for the individual and the city.... Likely it is that tyranny becomes established from no other system than democracy, the most complete and savage slavery arising from what I take to be the height of liberty.

We have noted that the democratic culture exalts the triad of pleasure, equality, and freedom. Freedom is necessary for the pursuit of pleasure, and equality is necessary to protect freedom. It is precisely here that Plato finds the inherently unstable nature of the democratic character and culture—its ultimate ambivalence toward law. On the one hand, in a democratic culture the rule of law exists to protect the freedom necessary for the pursuit of pleasure. On the other hand, law inevitably imposes limits on freedom, and thus on the pursuit of pleasure. We have seen that in a democratic culture the citizens, when "some restriction of any kind is introduced, they are vexed and refuse to bear it.... They wind up paying attention to none of the laws, written or unwritten, so that in no way shall anyone be ruler over them" (563de). When control of the "many-headed beast" is threatened, the "lion" may come to its assistance, and the emotion of anger is joined to the emotions associated with the pursuit of pleasure, anger toward anything or anyone who would say no to the "many-headed beast."

We may conclude this chapter with one quotation and an addendum. The quotation: "Then, just as a sick body needs only the slightest tilt from outside to be cast into distress, and sometimes without anything from outside is in rebellion against itself, so a city in a similar condition, from the slightest excuse ... becomes ill and fights with itself and sometime without any external cause is in rebellion against itself" (556e). The addendum: what Plato says here about the organized systems of the human body and the human polity is just as true of the organized system of the human soul. The law of (moral) entropy is a pervasive and inescapable feature of the cosmos.

11

THE DESIRES *of the* GOOD DIALECTICIAN

Courage (n.) "That quality of mind which shows itself in danger without fear or shrinking; bravery, boldness, valor."

Patience (n.) "The suffering or enduring (of pain, trouble, or evil) with calmness and composure. Forbearance, longsuffering, longanimity under provocation of any kind; esp. forbearance or bearing with others, their faults, limitations, etc."

Gentle (adj.) "Of persons: mild in disposition or behavior; kind, tender."

Magnanimity (n.) "Nobility of feeling; superiority to petty resentment or jealousy; generous disregard of injuries."

Docility (n.) "Aptness to be taught; readiness to receive instruction; teachableness."

Arrogance (n.) "The taking of too much upon oneself as one's right; the assertion of unwarrantable claims in respect to one's own importance; undue assumption of dignity, authority, or knowledge."

Moderate (trans. v.) "To abate the excessiveness of; to render less violent, intense, rigorous, or burdensome."

In this chapter we will finish our search for the traits of the good and effective dialectician. As noted in the conclusion to part 1, this third part deals with what may be called "moral" traits or features of desire. One may wonder about this focus on "features of desire." After all, is not the first trait of the good dialectician, a qualified researcher in the field of ethics, the possession of a strong desire to know the truth about the Big Picture? Yes it is, but that desire to know the truth is a desire that arises from the rational part of the soul, and so may be called a rational desire. The problem is, as we can see from the previous chapter, that the rational part may not always be in control of the nonrational part, "the soul" may not always in fact be governing "the body." When that happens, although there may be *some* rational desire to know the truth, that rational desire is weak and ineffective, overcome by one or other of the nonrational desires located either in the spirited part or in the appetitive part. The rational desire may be real and genuine when viewed in the abstract—of course we want to know the truth about the Big Picture—but when it comes to examine a particular concrete question, the genuine desire on the part of reason may vanish or become seriously weakened.

In chapter 9 we uncovered three types of goods that can be seen as goods desired by the nonrational parts: (1) honor, status, and power, desired by the "lion"; (2) wealth and possessions, desired by the "many-headed beast"; and (3) pleasure and sensual gratification, also desired by the "many-headed beast." In that chapter we also listed the central or cardinal virtues, features which must be present in the parts of the soul if it is to perform its function of governing "the body" effectively: *wisdom* in the rational part, *courage* in the spirited part, *self-control* or *moderation* in the appetitive (and also the spirited) part, and *justice*, a kind of virtue of the system in which each of the parts is left to perform its own function without being interfered with by any of the others.

The traits we considered in part 2 are simply necessary components of "wisdom." The first trait covered in part 1, as we just saw, refers to a desire of the rational part and so is to be placed there. The other four traits in part 1 undergird the first and pertain to the rational part as well. Thus, everything we have covered so far properly belongs only to the rational part of the soul. But as we saw from chapter 10, just because the rational part is otherwise in good shape, it does not follow that the soul itself is in good shape if the rational part is not in control of the nonrational parts of the soul, the spirited and appetitive parts. The traits we need to develop in order to complete our list are all going to be forms of what Plato called "courage" regarding the spirited part and "moderation," that is, agreement among the parts about which part (the reason) is to rule. We will divide "moderation" into two categories, moderation of the spirited part and moderation of the appetitive part. With that our investigation will have been completed. As we did in connection with the traits developed in parts 1 and 2, the defense of the traits we are about to uncover as indeed necessary features of the good dialectician will be reserved to the conclusion of part 3.

Traits Related to Moderation in the "Lion"

Remember that the spirited part is the part in the soul by which we get angry, become confrontational, get stirred up. The desire to win, to be superior, to have our way, to be liked—these are the desires of the spirited part, and they are not as such bad desires at all. People can do themselves and others serious harm when they do *not* get angry and stand up for what is right. So the problem with these desires arises not because we have them but because we do not have them in the right degree or for the right reasons.

Let us look at courage first. Two passages from the *Gorgias* will serve to illustrate the point. In chapter 7 we considered nine traits necessary for the good dialectician, the last of which was the trait of knowing what forms of refutation are "completely worthless with regard to the truth" (471e). Polus employed three such forms against Socrates: (1) "witnesses," the appeal to what people think; (2) "scaring," the expression of incredulity that anyone could be so foolish and pigheaded as to actually believe what is being asserted; and (3) laughter or mockery. The appeal to "witnesses" is not necessarily "completely worthless with respect to the truth," *provided* that the people summoned as witnesses are genuine experts regarding the topic under consideration. But all too often the people appealed to are not genuine experts on the topic at all, though they may be widely respected and thought so. It is the appeal to *these* non-experts that constitutes "refutation completely worthless as far as truth is concerned."

Now resisting these three types of refutation can require courage, which "shows itself in danger without fear or shrinking." And to what danger do these types of refutation expose a person? It is a "danger" that did not seem to bother Socrates one bit, but does in fact cause a lot of people to fear and shrink back. It is the fear of being laughed at or thought foolish or idiotic for holding the position one holds. The use of polls is a particularly illuminating illustration. Any poll showing that only a small percentage of people believe P supposedly leads to the conclusion that those who believe P are wrong. It takes courage to stick to your beliefs. This does not preclude looking for evidence to see where you have gone wrong, but it takes courage to hold unpopular views until they are proven to be false.

There is another danger which can cause people to shrink back from stating their beliefs, one related to the feeling of shame. In chapter 6 we saw Callicles's remarkable declaration: "luxury and licentiousness and liberty, if held in abundance, this is excellence and happiness" (492c). And how does Socrates react to this? With *commendation*, rather than condemnation. "Not at all ignobly, Callicles, do you prosecute the argument with such openness, for you are now saying clearly what others believe but do not wish to say. I beg you, then, not to slack off in any way, so that it may become perfectly clear how in truth we ought to live" (492d). Many people believe what Callicles says, but they shrink back from saying so because of shame; they fear what others would think of them if they knew their real beliefs. The many, then, are not good dialecticians; we need one another in the search for truth, but we do not need someone who will tailor his statements to fit the beliefs of others. Courage, or something much like it, is necessary for another reason (*Republic* 535b):

> S: We must search not only for those who possess noble and valiant characters but also for those with qualities in their nature contributing to this education.
>
> G: Will you explain what sort you have in mind?
>
> S: It is necessary, my blessed man, that they be most eager for their studies and learn them without difficulty, for human souls much more quickly shrink from difficult studies than from gymnastic training, because the labor is proper to the souls, something their own and not shared with the body.

Dialectic can be hard work; as Socrates says, it can make strenuous physical exercise look like child's play in comparison. A lot of people do not like hard intellectual work. It would be nice to approach tough intellectual questions with a keenness and zest for the task. Lacking that, the good dialectician must possess at least something resembling courage in his readiness to sustain the laborious effort dialectic sometimes demands.

And it is not only courage that is necessary. *Patience* is also required for three reasons. Socrates suggests that a solid training in dialectic should take about five years (539e). Not only is the labor heavy, it can be lengthy as well. The good dialectician will recognize that gaining a solid grasp of the truth may come only after long years of hard effort. Second, we have to learn to be patient with ourselves. We need to be ready to admit that we have taken false steps, devoting time and effort to following a line of thought that does not pay off. We may occasionally argue poorly, lose our cool, miss the obvious argument that should have been made, etc. Third, and just as important, we must learn to be patient with others rather than get angry with them. Even if well intentioned, not everyone can argue well, understand the principles of dialectic, or possess the traits of the good dialectician. When we find we are dealing with such a person lacking in the dialectical virtues (and we must never forget that we ourselves are always or nearly always just that kind of person), how shall we react? As Socrates does, with patience and understanding. It is helpful here to keep in mind the idea that people are trying to do the best they can, or at the very least it is helpful to suppose that they are and to act on that supposition. And if the person with whom we are speaking is trying to do the best he can but is mistaken (we think), then Socrates has some excellent advice for us.

One of the principal figures in the early part of the *Republic* besides Socrates is a man named Thrasymachus whose views somewhat resemble those of Callicles. Socrates had been discussing with others about how good and beneficial the practice of justice really is when Thrasymachus breaks in (336bc, 336e–337a):

> S: Thrasymachus had tried several times to take up the conversation while we were speaking, but whenever he did so he was prevented by the listeners who wished to hear the argument to its conclusion. But when we left off and I had said these things, no longer could he keep quiet but gathered himself together like a wild animal and came upon us as though to tear us to pieces. Polemarchus and I were frightened and struck with panic and he shouted in our midst:

T: What nonsense has had its grip on you two for so long, Socrates, and why do you act like simpletons towards one another, deferring to one another? ...

S: Do not be so hard on us, Thrasymachus, for if Polemarchus and I went astray somehow in our examination of the question, you must realize we did so unwillingly. Do you not think that if we were searching for gold, we would never willingly give way to each other in the search and so destroy the possibility of discovering it? And so, searching for justice as we now are, for something more valuable than much gold, would we so thoughtlessly give way to one another and not be deadly serious that this thing above all be found? You should look at it that way, my friend. And as for me, I think we simply are unable. It seems far more proper for us to be pitied by you clever people than to be dealt with harshly.

The virtues of courage and patience with others and with ourselves are greatly helped by the virtue of *magnanimity*, literally, the virtue of "greatness of soul." The opposed vice is pettiness, smallness of soul. The great-souled person looks at the world from a large perspective; he sees himself and his life from that perspective. He sees that whatever may happen to him that he himself did not bring about by his own actions is not really all that important in the large scheme of things. If he has acted well, that is all he asks. One of the Stoic philosophers was once threatened: "If you do not do such-and-such, I will kill you." The Stoic's response: "May it do you good." Socrates is a remarkable example of a great soul. The good dialectician will remain cool in an argument and patient with incomprehension and dislike because he possesses a great soul.

We will need to add another virtue to our list of traits of the good dialectician—the virtue of *honesty*, often translated as "frankness" or "candor." The good dialectician who possesses the first trait, a strong desire for the truth, will also be disposed toward honesty and frankness—saying exactly what he believes—but as we have seen he will also need courage in order to ensure that this disposition to say what he genuinely believes is not blocked by fear of somehow getting in trouble because of his frankness.

Socrates calls the courageous person the one whose "spirit preserves while experiencing pains and pleasures what has been handed down by the reasoning part concerning what is to be feared, what not" (*Republic* 442c). It is easy to see what Socrates means by preserving "what has been handed down by the reasoning part concerning what is to be feared, what not" in the midst of *pains*, but why does he add *pleasures* in the description of a virtue connected with the spirited element, the "lion," rather than with the "many-headed beast"? That is a good question, but we will delay answering it until we can turn to a consideration of the virtues related to moderation in the "many-headed beast." We have still to consider additional virtues related to moderation in the "lion."

Two virtues are quite important in this respect, the first of which could be called "humility," but that word is frequently misunderstood, so *docility* will be our preferred term. There is a second virtue which could also be covered by the word "humility" but is not the same thing as docility, and perhaps the awkward expression *absence of arrogance* will best serve our purpose. Docility and absence of arrogance are closely related but not identical. We have already encountered several instances of Socrates's docility; let us mention just one, perhaps the most striking. In chapter 4 we saw Socrates's declaration in the *Gorgias* of the kind of person he took himself to be (458ab):

> And what kind of a person am I? One of those who would gladly be refuted if I were to say something untrue, and gladly refute if someone else were to say something untrue, being not at all less pleased whether refuted or refuting. Because I count *this* the greater good, by the degree to which being released from the greatest evil is a greater good than to release someone else from it. I believe that nothing is so great an evil for a human being as false belief about the matters we happen to be speaking about now.

A lot of people like the truth and say that they want it, but they also like winning and being shown to be right. They may be presented with an excellent argument against their position but stubbornly refuse to admit their error, because what is at stake is not just the subject under discussion but also their sense of worth. They may bring up all kinds of spurious objections to the argument and defend their own position by a host of rationalizations and special pleadings. At the beginning of the *Republic,* a group of about half a dozen men catches up with Socrates and the young man Glaucon. The two have come down to the Piraeus, the port of Athens, and are just beginning their return to the city (327c):

> Polemarchus: Do you see us, how many we are?
>
> S: Of course.
>
> P: Well then, you must either show yourselves stronger than we or else remain here.
>
> S: But is there not one possibility left out, that we persuade you we must leave?
>
> P: But would you be able to persuade us if we do not listen?
>
> G: Of course not.
>
> P: Well, we are not going to listen; know that well.

People do not want to listen, will refuse to listen, for a variety of reasons. They may be afraid of what the argument may show them, or they may view arguments as a contest for superiority rather than as a means to the pursuit of truth. We first saw this latter point in connection with the timocratic character in the previous chapter. The spirited part wants to rule over the rational part and refuses to be under its control—there is lack of "moderation" in the lion.

Docility is a readiness, even a strong desire, to learn from whatever others might have to teach us. As we saw in part 1, I cannot search for something I already have. If I already possess thorough knowledge about some topic, I may be disinclined to listen to whatever you have to say. Why bother? But maybe, although I do genuinely have considerable knowledge of the topic, you might nonetheless be able to enlighten me about some useful point or offer me a somewhat different perspective. It may also be that I do not in fact possess the extensive knowledge I think I possess. In either case, there is something of an underestimation of the benefit I might receive from listening to you or an unwarranted assumption regarding the depth of knowledge I ascribe to myself. I am, to some degree, arrogant. In contrast, if any single trait could be said to be the defining feature of Socrates's life, it was his lack of arrogance, his claim to know nothing. And the primary instance of this lack of arrogance on the part of Socrates can be seen in our treatment of the *Apology* in chapter 4.

The key event in Socrates's life, as he tells it, was the answer given by the god Apollo to his dead friend Chaerephon's question—of all the humans now alive, no one is wiser than Socrates! We recall the passage quoted earlier (21b–d, 23ab):

> What is the god saying, and why does he speak in such riddles? As for myself, I recognize that no wisdom great or small belongs to me. Why then does he speak as he does, presenting me as the wisest of all? Surely he is not lying; that would not be right of him.... Well then, I gave a thorough examination to [someone Socrates does not name who was active in politics and had a reputation for wisdom] ... but after speaking with him he seemed to me to be a man who appeared wise to many others—and especially to himself—but in fact was not. Then I undertook to show him that although he thought himself wise he was not, and at this I became disliked by him and by many of the bystanders. But on departing I was saying to myself that yes, indeed, I was wiser than he. Probably neither of us knows anything excellent, but he, ignorant as he was, believed himself to know things, whereas I, since I did not know, did not think I knew. So perhaps by this little bit I was indeed wiser than he, since the things I did not know I did not think I knew.... It is likely, men [of the Athenian jury], that in truth

god is wise, and by this oracle he is saying that human wisdom is worth little or nothing. He seems when he mentions Socrates to be but using my name, citing me as an example, as if he would say: "O men, that man is the wisest who, like Socrates, has come to know that in respect of wisdom he is in truth worthy of nothing."

Lack of arrogance, no undue claim to knowledge, is a necessary condition for docility, a strong desire to learn from anyone who may have something to teach us. It is impossible to be open to learning from others if I am unwarrantedly sure of my own knowledge. The two virtues, though different, are closely linked. And although the following remark may be only "true enough to be worth saying," it nonetheless does seem to be worth saying. It takes something of a large soul to avoid an "undue assumption of dignity, authority, or knowledge."

Before Callicles makes his wonderful speech about "luxury and licentiousness and liberty," he delivers another in which he advises Socrates to give up the life of philosophy and refutation and devote himself rather to the active life of politics and civic affairs. Callicles's speech ends as follows (486cd):

> Take my advice, my good man; stop this refuting business and engage in the accomplishments of the active life, engage in practices from which you will acquire the reputation for having smarts, and leave these neat toys to others, whether we must call them frivolity or even silliness, because of which you will dwell in empty houses, and be not envious of those engaging in refutation over such trivial matters but of those who possess life and fame and many other goods.

Once again, Socrates is by no means ungrateful to Callicles for his words because he sees that Callicles has displayed *good will* towards him (487cd):

> And what sure sign do I have? I will tell you. I know, Callicles, that there are four of you who have become partners in wisdom.... Once I overheard you

[the four "partners"] deliberating regarding up to what point wisdom was to be cultivated, and I also know that some opinion like this was gaining the victory among you: not to engage eagerly in philosophy all the way to precision, but you were encouraging one another to take care lest, becoming wiser than necessary, you destroy yourselves unawares. So because I hear you advising me what you advised your companions, I have sufficient evidence that you truly are well disposed toward me.

To possess good will toward someone is to act as one would toward a "companion," a friend. It is easy to view my dialectical opponent as an enemy to be defeated. I confess I find it quite difficult to view that person as I would a friend, a person whose welfare is bound up with mine, a person for whom I wish good things. The point of dialectical argument, after all, *should* be that of a *shared* search for the truth, a truth which is a common good for both of us, for "nothing is so great an evil for a human being as false belief about the matters we happen to be speaking about now" (458ab). The virtues of docility and good will go hand in hand. In fact, good will is a significant contributor to docility: if I see us as (potential) friends engaging in a collaborative endeavor for common benefit, then I am prepared to look upon you not as an adversary striving for victory but as a friend trying to straighten me out and correct my false (and therefore harmful) belief. Now of course, not all the people with whom we enter into dialectical exchanges in fact have the friendly attitude of good will toward us; they may be trying to show off, win, put us down, show how foolish our view is, etc. But we are not talking about *them*, are we?

A person of good will practices what has been called the principle of charity: to try to place the best interpretation on a person's remarks. Rather than seeking to trip up an opponent by using his own words, a person of good will seeks to discover what the other person really meant to convey by the words used. Sometimes people are not good at expressing themselves clearly or putting their beliefs in the most plausible light possible. It is the task of the good dialectician not only to understand what was *said* but also to understand what was *meant*. The search for truth is seldom well served by focusing exclusively on the (perhaps misleading or otherwise imperfect) statement of a position or argument.

A person of good will also possesses the trait of *fairness* or *impartiality*. The other person's position and arguments are examined as he would his own. He looks for the strong points in the other's position, and he will not conceal weaknesses in his own position. He assesses the evidence for and against both positions in the same manner. In weighing the merits of the competing arguments, he does not fudge the issue by placing his thumb on either side. He follows the "Golden Rule," treating the other person and his position and arguments as he himself would want to be treated.

Just engage in this thought experiment: what would it be like if I genuinely saw others as friends, striving to help me out, set me straight, correct my error as they see it? What difference would that make? I might be unable to convince him or help him, but I can say I tried to do so in the most effective way possible for showing people their error—by treating them as friends and not as fools. He might be unable to convince me, perhaps because of his own ignorance or perhaps because of mine; either way, he tried, and I will take that as an act of a friend. Good will is an essential virtue of the good dialectician.

Traits Related to Moderation in the "Many-Headed Beast"

"The many-headed beast," the appetitive part of the soul, as we have seen, possesses two different sorts of desires: desire for things that are useful and desire for things that are pleasant to the senses.

Correspondingly, there are two forms of unjust character: the oligarchic character regarding desires of the first sort, and the democratic character regarding desires of the second. Moderation would be a virtue of both kinds of desires in which both aspects of the "many-headed beast" are subject to the rational part. Since the time of Aristotle, Plato's foremost student, it has been customary to distinguish these two forms of moderation by two names—generosity or liberality, related to the desire for things useful for other purposes, and temperance, related to the desires for sensual pleasures. The upcoming discussion, then, could work with this distinction between the two kinds of desires, but I think for our purposes we will not need to uncover the traits of a good dialectician by considering these two kinds of desires separately. We will treat the two kinds of desires together, highlighting one or the other as seems useful.

"A person should not be a judge in his own case." People are encouraged, in both formal and informal contexts, to disqualify themselves from rendering a decision or judgment if they are subject to a conflict of interest. Why is this? Simply put, people typically find it extremely difficult if not impossible to render a fair judgment when they are a party to the decision, that is, when their own interests will be affected by their decision. They are often called upon to recuse themselves, that is, to disqualify themselves as judges in a particular case.

Now, when an ordinary person must make a decision regarding how he should act, he may and frequently does find himself as an interested party to the case/decision and faced with a conflict of interest, even when there are no other persons affected by his decision, at least in any obvious way. This can happen whenever there is some lack of *justice* in the person's soul, whenever there is not complete agreement about "who" should rule, that is, whenever the nonrational parts of the soul are not perfectly subjected to the rational and usurp the rational part's proper functioning. Whenever there is not this perfect subjection, the parts of the soul become parties, and, as Socrates notes, there comes to be something like a civil war among the various parts: "So is it not necessary that there be a kind of sedition among these three things [the man, the lion, the many-headed beast], an interfering and meddling and uprising of one part against the whole of the soul in order that it rule within it in an unfitting manner, since its nature is such that it befits it to serve as a slave?" (*Republic* 444b).

When Socrates speaks of their "interfering and meddling and uprising," he is thinking principally of the nonrational parts' interference with the function of the rational part, the function of control and direction. Each of the two nonrational parts are such that "by nature it befits it to serve as slave" to the rational part. This talk of "slave" will sound harsh to modern ears. All Socrates means is that it is befitting to the nonrational parts, it is proper and better for them, part of their function, to be under the subjection, rule, and guidance of the rational part; and this is so because of the nature that the nonrational parts possess. These parts are *unable by nature to be adequate judges of the true good*, since *by their nature they are incapable of recognizing long-term benefit and harm*, a recognition or awareness which is possessed only by the rational part. It is the awareness by the rational part of long-term benefit and harm that justifies the rational part's function as ruler, and it is the lack of this awareness by the nonrational parts that justifies their function as ruled. It is in their best interest to be so subjected, and when they are not, then their own self-direction and control, far from being beneficial to those parts, in fact turns out to be damaging and destructive for them and for the person as a whole. It is also possible for the rational part to so dominate and repress the other, nonrational parts as to deny them their legitimate function, expression, and needs. This typically occurs, though, because *something else* is out of balance in the non-rational parts.

In part 2, we defended two traits of the good dialectician: readiness to attend to the possibility of systematic interconnections among the features of the cosmos (and the ability to note those interconnections where they exist), and the appreciation of the importance of long-term and short-term consequences. Having defended the appropriateness of those two traits, we have *ipso facto* defended the correctness of the subjection of the non-rational to the rational part. When a person faces a decision about how he should act and his soul lacks perfect justice and the parts of the soul have become parties, he may fail to identify himself with his entire soul; he may identify himself (falsely) with the lion or with either aspect of the many-headed beast, and the body takes on governance over (and away from) the soul. The good dialectician will recognize this as a constant danger and will take all steps possible to guard against it.

In our treatment of the virtue of courage we noted Socrates's remark that "spirit preserves while experiencing pains and pleasures what has been handed down by the reasoning part concerning what is to be feared, what not" (*Republic* 442c), and we raised the question then of why courage should be about *pleasures* in addition to pains. We are now ready to address that question. In the *Republic*, Socrates makes an absolutely essential point regarding what he calls "the departing of a belief from the mind," and in doing so employs some ideas discussed in chapter 2. In the following passage Socrates is concerned with overseeing the education of those who will be able to function effectively as guardians of the just community. Pupils, guardians in training, will need to be watched closely to ensure that their education is proceeding as it should (412e–413a):

S: It seems to me that they must be overseen at every stage of their lives, whether they are guardians of this teaching, and neither bewitched nor forced and inadvertently cast out [literally "exile"] this belief, the necessity of doing what is best for the city.

G: What do you mean by "casting out"?

S: I will tell you. It seems to me that the departure of a belief from the mind may be voluntary or involuntary—voluntary for the departure of false belief of the person learning differently, and involuntary for the departure of every true belief.

G: I understand about the voluntary, but I need further instruction about the involuntary.

S: Do you not think that that men are unwillingly stripped of good things but willingly of evil things? Or is it not an evil to be mistaken about the truth and a good to possess the truth? And does it not seem to you that to believe the things that are is to possess the truth?

G: But of course you are right, and those seem to me to be unwilling who have been stripped of true belief.

Socrates's talk of a belief's "departing from the mind" is simply a way of referring to the fact that a person has changed his mind. I once believed P but I now no longer believe it; I have changed my mind about P; belief in P has "departed from my mind." Now we saw in chapter 2 why true beliefs are good things and false beliefs are bad things. True beliefs are a reasonably accurate picture of reality and false beliefs are a distorted picture, and successful action depends upon our possessing accurate rather than distorted pictures. We want good things and true beliefs are good things, so we want true beliefs. We wish to avoid bad things and false beliefs are bad things, so we wish to avoid false beliefs. Thus, when we replace a false belief with a true belief, a false belief has departed our mind and a true belief has entered, and we have replaced something bad with something good. Doing that is good, and we want it to happen. But when we replace a true belief with a false belief, we have replaced something good with something bad, which we do not want to happen. Why then does this second exchange ever occur? A very good question (413bc):

> S: And do they not suffer this when they have been stolen from or bewitched or forced?
>
> G: Now again I do not understand.
>
> S: Perhaps I am speaking in the style of a composer of tragedies. By those stolen from I mean those who have been won over by argument and those who have forgotten, because in some cases by time, in other cases by argument, their belief has been taken from them unawares.... By those forced I mean those for whom some pain or suffering produces a change of mind.... And by those bewitched I mean, as I think you also would say, those who change their belief, having been enchanted by some pleasure or terrified by some fear.

This is an extraordinarily important passage, for in it Socrates provides an answer to the question of why anyone would ever trade a true belief for a false belief, or more precisely, why anyone would ever hold a false belief about an important matter where the falsity is not all that difficult to discern. The first part of Socrates's answer is that no one would ever voluntarily substitute a false belief for a true belief, at least if he fully recognized what was at stake. Since no one would ever want this to happen, when it does occur it must be something involuntary and against the person's wishes. It occurs in one of three ways: either through (1) "being stolen," when a (presumably bad) argument "slips" the true belief out of his mind; or through (2) "being forced" when some pain or suffering "compels" the person to change his mind; or through (3) "being bewitched" when the enchantment of some pleasure or the terror of some fear of lost pleasure "beguiles" him to change his mind.

I think (1) is quite clear. You can be fooled into believing what is false by a bad argument or by lies; in such a case, your true belief has been stolen from you. We study logic in order to avoid being tricked and deceived in this way. However, (2) is a bit harder to see. Socrates speaks of "being forced" when "people change their minds because of some pain or suffering." Now what does this mean? You believe that two and two equal four, and I want you to believe that they equal five instead. I pick up a baseball bat and make ready to swing and say: "If you do not believe that two and two equal five, I will bash your brains out." Now I may be able to force you to *say* that two and two equal five, but it is hard to see how I am going to be able to force you to *believe* it. Just how is this compulsion supposed to work?

Well, it is really not all that hard to answer this question; I think every one of us has had many opportunities to experience this firsthand. You need to exercise, right? Of course you do. Exercise is a good thing, right? So you are going to go over to the gym every day after work and put in a good hour's worth of exercise. Well, that was six weeks ago and I meet up with you again and ask how your exercise plan is going and you say, well, you tried it for a bit but decided you did not really need all that exercise after all, and you are doing just fine without it. This happens all the time. Now were you "compelled" or "forced" to change your belief about the importance of exercise? Not really, but at the same time it is not at all odd to think that the difficulty (or pain) associated with holding and acting on a belief might very well cause a person to change his mind regarding that belief. And if the first belief were true and his new belief false, then he would have been subjected to what in this context Socrates calls "force." Using such language is not intended to suggest that the person is not responsible or in some way to blame for changing his mind; that is a different question. Here we are only trying to explain why persons now hold false beliefs when before they held true ones. (These remarks provide another reason for the importance of courage.)

Once you see how "force" works, it is easy to see how "bewitchment" works as well. The only difference between them is that in place of the *pain* or evil associated with holding and acting on a true belief, we substitute either the *pleasure* or other good associated with holding and acting on a false belief or the fear of lost pleasure or good associated with acting on a true belief. The absence of a strongly desired pleasure can mean the presence of a strongly undesired pain (unpleasant feeling, unsatisfied craving, etc.). Cigarette smoking is bad for you, right? You are going to give it up right now, are you not? So I meet you six weeks later and ask how things are going with your quitting, and you say that you are young and healthy and you will give up smoking some day when you are a bit older, but smoking for a while longer is not going to do you that much harm. People can begin their lives believing that some action, like smoking, is bad and wrong but then start performing the action because it is pleasant and then often find themselves believing after a while that the action really is not that bad after all, and what do other people know about it anyway. "Bewitchment"? Well, of course it depends on whether or not the original belief was true or false, whether the change from the first to the second belief was voluntary or involuntary. It would be "bewitchment" if the original belief were true and the current belief false. It can happen.

So we can now see what Socrates meant with respect to courage when he said that "spirit preserves while experiencing pains and pleasures what has been handed down by the reasoning part concerning what is to be feared, what not" (442c). Socrates is talking about preserving true beliefs under the attack by "force" (pains) or "bewitchment" (pleasures). For the sake of precision, I think Socrates might do better to restrict a virtue of the "lion," the spirited part, to the preserving of true beliefs in the midst of pains and other fearful things that touch on the goods of the spirited part, and leave it to a virtue of the "many-headed beast," the appetitive part, to the preserving of true beliefs in the midst of sensual pleasures and other goods of the appetitive part. But whether or not we make these modifications does not matter; the sole point is to get this vital idea out on the table.

A bit later on in the *Republic* Socrates uses this striking image, still speaking about proper education for those who will at some point assume the role of guardians of the city where justice abounds (429d–430b):

> You know that when dyers wish to dye wool so as to retain the purple color, they first select from the various colors of wool only the wool that is white in its nature and then give it preparatory treatment, taking care by various measures that it take on the brightness of the color in the best way, and only then do they immerse the wool in the dying liquid. And material dyed in this manner becomes firm-fast and washing with or without soap cannot remove the sheen of the colors.... So understand that in a similar way we were striving to the best of our ability when we selected soldiers [guardians of the just city] and educated them with harmony and gymnastics. The sole point of our scheme was nothing other than that having been convinced, guardians should receive the laws like dye in order that their belief become firm-fast about the things to be feared and other matters, and to hold on to that belief owing to their suitable nature and training, and that these detergents not wash out of them this dye of theirs, terribly effective detergents in washing away, pleasure more powerful in achieving this than any washing powder, and pain and fear and desire more effective than any soap. This power, this preservation, whatever may come, of the upright and lawful belief concerning things to be feared and things not, this is what I call and assert to be courage.

What Socrates is getting at is "moderation" in any of the non-rational parts of the soul—whether in the "lion" or in either part of the "many-headed beast"—an obedience and subjection to the rational and properly ruling part of the soul. In fact, we can be so attached to the goods of the spirited part (honor, status, power) or to the goods of the appetitive part (wealth, sensual pleasures) that we are blinded by fear and "force" or seduced by the magic of "bewitchment," and we surrender our true beliefs or never acquire them because of the cost to one of the non-rational parties with which we thereby become effectively identified.

We saw this idea of the rational part's being blinded by pains or seduced by pleasures expressed briefly in a passage from the *Phaedo*: "The soul reasons best when nothing of such things [information from the senses] disturbs it, neither hearing nor sight nor pain nor pleasure, but when it is most itself by itself, dismissing the body and as much as possible not associating with it or being affected by it as it stretches out toward reality" (65c). The senses can be a hindrance to discerning the ordered structure of reality, but it is not the senses alone that can pose a problem in this regard. Sensual desires can also obscure the recognition of this order. A second passage in the *Phaedo* reinforces this point and carries it further (82d–83d):

> S: Lovers of knowledge know, when philosophy has taken hold of their soul, that it has been thoroughly bound and fastened in the body, compelled to view the things that are through the body as through a jail cell and not through itself, rolling about in total ignorance. And philosophy also understands fully that *the most frightful thing about this imprisonment is that it comes about through the soul's own desires, so that the bound person himself is the chief accomplice in his own binding*. So as I was saying, the lovers of knowledge know that when philosophy has taken hold of their soul it softly speaks encouraging words to the soul and endeavors to set it free.... The soul of the true philosopher believes that it must not resist this opportunity for release, and as far as possible removes itself from pleasures and desires and pains and fears, considering that whenever someone is excessively pleased or pained or afraid or desirous of something, he suffers from doing so none of the evils one might suppose, such as disease or the expense of gratifying one's appetite, but what is the greatest and ultimate of all evils, this he suffers and fails to recognize.

Cebes: And what is that, Socrates?

S: The soul of every man, whenever it is very much pleased or pained, is compelled to believe that the very thing from which it derives such powerful feeling is the most distinct and truest of beings, which it certainly is not. And this is especially the case with visible things, or not? ... So, in this sort of experience, is it not that the soul is most especially bound by the body? ... Since every pleasure or pain has something like a nail and nails the soul to the body and impedes it and makes it body-like, believing to be true whatever the body might say.

Let us look at some examples of the possibility of this binding or blinding. The *Crito* is a dialogue set between the *Apology* and the *Phaedo*, set between Socrates's trial and his execution. Socrates's close friend Crito has come to visit him in prison, to inform him that he will likely be executed on the following day and to beg Socrates to allow him and Socrates's other friends to rescue him from prison before the sentence of death is carried out (45d–46c):

C: I am ashamed both for you and for us, your friends, lest everything that has happened to you be thought to have occurred because of our cowardice: the bringing of your case to court when it was not necessary at all, and then the very conduct of the trial as it developed, and then this finish, a completely ridiculous affair—all this will seem to have escaped our control owing to our incompetence and cowardice, we who did not rescue you or you yourself, which we [Socrates and his friends] could have done had we been of the slightest use. Look, Socrates, and examine whether this is not something both evil and shameful for you and for us. But come, take counsel, or rather, it's no longer time to take counsel but to have taken counsel already, and there is only one counsel. Everything must be done tonight. If we still delay, everything becomes impossible and nothing can be done. But by all means, Socrates, follow my advice and do not deviate one bit.

S: My dear Crito, your eagerness would be worth much if it were joined with sound advice, but if it is not, then *how much the greater, so much the more difficult to deal with*. It is necessary, then, for us to examine whether we should do what you advise, or not. Because I not only now but ever have been the kind of person to follow nothing other than the argument which seems to my reason to be the best. I cannot disregard the arguments I made earlier now that events have turned out as they have. They seem to me to hold pretty much the same, and I respect and hold them in regard as I did before, and be assured that if we can find nothing better to say now, I will not agree with you, even if the power of the current majority should frighten us like children, hurling imprisonments and deaths and confiscations of property. How, then, shall we best examine these matters in the most measured manner?

In the *Phaedo*, the dialogue which takes place on the day of Socrates's death, Socrates presents an argument for the immortality of the soul; this argument is then opposed by two counter-arguments, and then Socrates presents his masterful critique of misology we examined in chapter 5. Immediately after that passage, Socrates offers the following remarks regarding how he and his friends should conduct themselves. His comments, as he faces death, can serve as a lesson for all of us (91a–c):

I am at risk of not maintaining a philosophical attitude on the present topic [the soul's immortality and the argument for it] but of striving to win, like those who are poorly educated. They, whenever there is some disagreement, give no thought to pursuing the truth of the matter but rather are most eager to make their claims appear correct to the audience. And I seem to myself regarding this present matter to be very much like one of them, though I differ in one respect. I will not be so eager that the arguments I am making seem correct to the bystanders, except perhaps as an incidental effect, but I am in dead earnest that the things I have said seem true to me. I am reasoning here, my dear friend—you can see how greedy I am for advantage—that if the things I am asserting turn out to be true, how admirable it is to be persuaded! But if there is nothing left for the dead person, then for this present time before death I will be less bothersome to my companions with my wailing, and my own folly will not survive long—that would indeed be something bad—but will perish just a little bit later. Having so prepared myself, Simmias and Cebes [the two who presented arguments against immortality], I come to confront your argument. But you two take my advice, thinking little about Socrates but much more about the truth. If I seem to you to be saying something true, agree with me; if not, oppose with every argument, *being careful lest from my own eagerness I deceive both myself and you*, and I depart like a bee leaving its sting.

Socrates, assuming he is to some extent a normal human being, would very much want to believe that escaping from prison is the right thing to do or that there is a life awaiting him after death. But he was acutely aware of the fact that we can very much want something to be true when it simply is not. So which desire is going to win out, the desire for the truth or the desire for the something else?

In the *Protagoras*, Socrates makes a striking point (333bc):

> S: Does a person acting unjustly seem to you to act sensibly because he acts unjustly?
>
> P: I would be ashamed, Socrates, to agree on this point, though many people do say so.
>
> S: Then shall I address my argument to them or to you?
>
> P: If you wish, argue first against the position of the many.
>
> S: It does not make any difference to me as long as you provide the answers, whether they seem to you to be true or not, because I am principally interested in scrutinizing the argument, though it may happen that *both I the questioner and the respondent are scrutinized as well.*

The dialectical exchange is of course an examination of an argument, a position. But as Socrates sees it, the exchange can also turn out to be an examination of the *participants themselves*, the kind of people they are, their character, the virtues/vices they possess, the seriousness of their commitment to the truth. In the previous chapter we quoted the English poet Ben Jonson, "Language most shows a man, speak that I may see thee." One might add, "Argue that I may see thee."

In chapter 8 we saw Socrates's appeal to the existence of an all-encompassing cosmic order which forms the backdrop against which Callicles's claims regarding the excellent and outstanding life must be evaluated. Callicles, remember, had asserted that, "in truth, Socrates, which you claim to pursue, here it is: luxury and licentiousness and liberty, if held in abundance, this is excellence and happiness" (*Gorgias* 492c). But this kind of life advocated by Callicles is the life of a brigand who "could be dear neither to another man nor to a god, for he could not be a partner, and wherever there is no partnership there's no friendship.... Partnership and friendship and self-control and things orderly and just hold together heaven and earth, gods and men, and because of this [wise men] call the whole of reality a cosmos, my friend, and not something disordered and uncontrolled" (507e–508a). Socrates asserts, as we saw, that Callicles's missing this absolutely crucial point relates to his having neglected geometry.

But Callicles can recognize some kinds of order. He can recognize the order of logical argument, can see that certain things he has said logically entail certain undesirable (to him) conclusions, and he struggles to escape the logical net Socrates weaves for him. He can see all that, but he cannot see the cosmic order toward which Socrates is pointing. Why can he not see that, always assuming of course that there is in fact such an order there to be seen? A possibility is that Callicles is blinded by his pleasures and pains, the desires of "the lion" or "the many-headed beast" or both. Perhaps Socrates is right, and our strong pleasures and pains act as nails which "nail the soul to the body and impede it and make it body-like, believing to be true whatever the body might say" (*Phaedo* 83d). And perhaps Callicles's soul indeed "has been thoroughly bound and fastened in the body, compelled to view the things that are through the body as through a jail cell and not through itself, rolling about in total ignorance" (82e). And perhaps this imprisonment of Callicles's soul does indeed "come about through Callicles's own desires, so that he himself is the chief accomplice in his own binding" (82e). Just how much does Callicles really want the truth? Does he want it more than the "luxury and licentiousness and liberty" to gratify whatever desires he happens to have? It is possible that Callicles does want to be blinded, to be imprisoned by his desires, or, at least, that at some level he prefers to be blinded rather than see the truth and all it entails. Almost all of us say we want the truth, but do we want it enough? And just how much, do we suppose, is *enough*?

The Danish philosopher and theologian Søren Kierkegaard (1813–55) wrote a book entitled *Purity of Heart Is to Will One Thing*. Taking our cue from Kierkegaard, let us call the virtue needed by the qualified researcher in ethics *purity of heart*, and let us define it as willing one thing. And what is the "one thing" willed by the qualified researcher, the good dialectician? Answer: the truth, the whole truth, and nothing but the truth about the moral topic in question.

The virtue of purity of heart is implied in the first trait of the good dialectician presented in the conclusion to part 1: "A strong desire to know the truth about the Big Picture." But what we did not point out in part 1 was the difficulty people face in possessing and exercising this strong desire to know the truth. I characterize this strong desire, this "purity of heart," as *resolutely setting one's will to know the truth no matter what cost that truth imposes on oneself or others.* This resolute setting of one's will to know the truth is no easy matter; it is not one of reciting a formula, or even of reciting it in a genuine and sincere and non-hypocritical way. It is easy to *say* I want the truth no matter what the cost it may pose for me, but it is by no means easy to really mean it and to put this desire into practice. The acquisition of purity of heart is a process, and it is not gained overnight, and there may be few who possess it deeply. The possession of purity of heart is a matter of degree; its possession can grow, and more importantly, it can ebb.

The cost to oneself, as we have seen, can take the form of some evil threatened or good lost for ourselves if we were to recognize the truth about a particular matter. The cost often comes in the form of pleasure foregone, pleasure we could have experienced had we held to a false belief. We can also be particularly biased regarding close friends or people for whom we have some reason to feel love or pity. Our discovering the truth may pose a similar and sometimes considerable cost for them. All of these considerations may need to be set aside, and *resolutely* set aside, if we are to discover the truth. The point here is not that when searching for the truth we should disregard the costs to ourselves and others of acting in a particular way. In fact, the truth about how to act may very well depend precisely on the costs of certain actions to ourselves or others. Why should we ignore the consequences of actions? The answer, of course, is that we should not. The problem arises not because those consequences are taken into consideration but because they are given an undue weight, and they are given an undue weight because of our *excessive* focus on or attachment to the desires coming either from the "lion" or from the "many-headed beast." The body is then in control of the soul. When the soul is in control of the body, then it is that the costs are assigned an *appropriate* weight. It is not the weighing that is bad, but rather the *misweighing* which stems from injustice in the soul, from a disordered and disorganized soul unable to perform its function of control in a proper manner.

Although purity of heart is implied in the first trait, "a strong desire to know the truth about the Big Picture," it is also closely related to the traits mentioned in this chapter. Without these latter traits purity of heart, even when genuine, is likely to be ineffective. Even if at some level I genuinely do wish for the truth about ethics (assuming of course always that there is or might be such a truth to be discovered), I am unlikely to discover that truth if I do not possess the traits discussed in this chapter. On the other hand, without purity of heart, I am most unlikely to possess these traits. Purity of heart and these other traits are mutually reinforcing. The possession of purity of heart does not guarantee, of course, that I *will* know the truth about a particular matter, but it can have this as its ultimate result. As purity of heart grows, I become more open to the discovery of the truth than I once was. The acquisition of purity of heart, although not the turning on of a light which immediately discloses the truth, is nonetheless a deliberate and willful turning of the eyes of the mind toward the truth which may be there to be discovered, a change in my openness to see whatever is there to be seen.

If purity of heart is a genuine openness to the truth, then its opposed vice, an unwillingness to recognize the truth, may be called "hardness of heart." This vice, besides rendering me less capable of recognizing the truth I might otherwise have recognized, has another important consequence. It makes me responsible, blameworthy, *both* for my mistaken belief that results from my hardness of heart *and* for the harmful consequences that arise from my acting on that mistaken belief. The reason for this is that responsibility and blameworthiness depend upon what is under a person's control. We like to think that if I am acting with a clear conscience, then everything is okay, but everything is *not* okay. First, if my conscience, my belief, is in fact mistaken, then I am acting on the basis of a false and inaccurate map of reality. When I act on the basis of a mistaken and false map, I am not very likely to get where I want to go. Second, if my conscience is in fact mistaken and the mistake arises from some hardness of heart, then I am to blame both for my ignorance (which is to some degree under my control) *and* for the bad consequences that can result from that ignorance. If I do not want to know whether it is your hamburger I am eating, then I cannot very well plead ignorance as a genuine excuse for having done so. On the one hand, I really did not know I was eating your hamburger; on the other hand, I did not take the trouble to find out whether it was yours. Under circumstances of this sort, the appeal to ignorance is a dodge, and it is a dodge that does not work for avoiding either the damage done or the *blame* for the damage done.

Let us conclude this chapter by recapitulating the traits we have uncovered as necessary for the good dialectician. We will provide a revised ordering and a defense of them in the conclusion to part 3:

courage: the quality of mind by which the dialectician faces danger or evil without shrinking back. This evil may take one of three forms: (a) disrespect or disesteem from others, (b) the sustaining of some damage or the loss of some good, (c) difficulty of the dialectical process itself;

patience: the quality of mind by which the dialectician endures some evil with calmness and composure. This evil may take one of three forms: (a) length of the dialectical process itself, (b) shortcomings in ourselves, (c) shortcomings in the person whom we encounter in the process;

gentleness: the quality of mind by which the dialectician is mild and kind toward the person with whom he is engaged in dialectic;

magnanimity: the quality of mind by which the dialectician rises above petty resentment and disregards insults or displays of ill-temper from others;

honesty: the quality of mind by which the dialectician is open and candid about his own beliefs;

docility: the quality of mind by which the dialectician desires to receive instruction from others. Such instruction may involve the correction of his own errors;

lack of arrogance: the quality of mind by which the dialectician makes no undue assumption of knowledge;

good will: the quality of mind by which the dialectician is concerned for the well being of the person with whom he is engaged in dialectic, especially as the other person's well being relates to his knowing the truth;

charity: the quality of mind by which the dialectician is concerned to understand the other person's point of view and the reasons that could be offered for his position;

fairness: the quality of mind by which the dialectician is impartial or equitable in his assessment of positions, treating all evidence, for or against, in a similar and consistent manner; and

moderation: the quality of mind by which the desires of the spirited and appetitive parts of the dialectician's soul are subjected to the rational part. The acquisition and retention of true beliefs are undermined neither by "force" (evils and pains) nor by "bewitchment" (goods and pleasures).

CONCLUSION *to* PART 3

Placing Order in the Dialectician's Soul

The first thing we are going to have to do is introduce modifications in two of the traits developed prior to part 3. From part 1, "a strong desire to search for the truth about the Big Picture," and from part 2, "the ability to focus on order and causal connections without being distracted by excessive attention to similarities and dissimilarities obvious to the senses." Regarding the trait from part 2, it is true that features striking to the senses can distract our thought from discovering the order and causal relationships among realities, but the senses can also distract in the powerful manner discussed in chapters 9, 10, and 11. The concept of purity of heart bears strongly on the trait from part 1, so we will provide a revision of that, as well. The two traits (suitably revised) are (1) purity of heart, a resolute willingness to search for the truth about the Big Picture no matter what the cost that truth imposes on oneself or others; and (2) the ability to focus on order and causal connections without being distracted either by excessive attention to similarities and dissimilarities obvious to the senses or by the pleasures and pains of the nonrational parts of the soul.

We can add to these the traits uncovered in chapter 11, all of which can be classed under (3) moderation in the "spirited" part of the soul—courage, honesty, patience, magnanimity, lack of arrogance, docility, gentleness, good will, charity, and fairness. Finally, we need a companion trait (4): moderation in the "appetitive" part of the soul—an effective readiness to subject the desires of the appetitive part of the soul to the rational part, so that the assessments by reason are not obscured or distorted by the desire for pleasure or possessions. We now turn to a general defense of these four traits, both new and revised. The condition, remember, is that everyone must agree upon the required traits of a qualified researcher, even those who lack the trait in question.

Each of the traits is necessary for the qualified researcher, the good dialectician, in the field of ethics simply in order to protect the researcher from his own biases and preferences. Although the truth is often the way I want it to be, this is not always the case. In some instances of the truth's not being the way I would like it to be, the facts of the matter are just too intrusive for me to be able to deny them. I do not *want* it to be true that I have a compound fracture of my right leg, but there it is and I could not persuade myself otherwise if I tried. But not all truths are such. Do I have cancer? Am I not fitted for my job? Is my spouse unfaithful? Are my children performing poorly at school? Now there, though the truth may be available to me if I want it, I may not want it, and not wanting it, I may remain ignorant.

In all fields of research the problem of "confirmation bias" rears its ugly head. In my research, I may want some theory to be true; with that desire for its truth, I may begin looking for evidence that would support my pet theory and turn away from or ignore or discount evidence in front of me pointing to the theory's falsity. Different people have different pets. For some it is their theories, for others their lifestyle, for others their political or religious group or a particular person, etc. Partiality is a feature endemic to the human condition, and no one is immune from it. Even someone who in fact does not possess those traits (and I for one think of myself as possessing them only in a rudimentary way if at all) but who recognizes that the truth is not always what one would want it to be, will also recognize the necessity of these traits for the qualified researcher in the field of ethics.

Thus the overall task of this book has been achieved. We have arrived at a definition of a qualified researcher in the field of ethics by specifying a set of traits which such a researcher must possess. Although different people might construct lists of traits that are superficially different, I believe that any adequate list would pretty much resemble any other. And if universal agreement is an indicator of truth, we have also provided an argument for the truth of requiring those traits. We have argued that *everyone*, even those who lack those traits themselves, will agree that *if* there is a truth to be discovered about the Big Picture, how best to live, those possessing the complete set of traits will be the ones best able to discover it.

Where does this leave us? We recall the argument from unresolved widespread disagreement presented in the introduction—namely, that there is no such thing as truth about ethics (truth about the Big Picture, the best life I can possibly live) because there is no agreement among those who think about the topic. If there were a truth, there should be at least *some* agreement, somewhere, but there is not, so we may reasonably conclude that there is no such truth.

In order to respond to this argument, we introduced the distinction between qualified and unqualified researchers in a particular field. A qualified researcher we defined as a person possessing all the traits necessary to discover the truth in that field, assuming that there is in fact a truth there to be discovered. In contrast, an unqualified researcher is a person who lacks one or more of those traits. The reason for introducing that distinction was to undermine the force of the argument from unresolved widespread disagreement. On the one hand, it is quite true that *if* there seemed to be no consensus at all among qualified researchers on any of the topics under discussion in that field, then we would have a good reason for believing that there just was no truth to be had in that field. But, on the other hand, if the lack of consensus belonged to unqualified researchers, the manifest fact of their unresolved and seemingly unresolvable differences in no way provides a reason for thinking there is no truth to be had.

Fair enough, but then the objection was raised: it is question begging within the field of ethics to stipulate who is or who is not a qualified researcher. In order to refute that objection, I wrote this book. It is not question begging to cite these traits as necessary for the qualified researcher, because the necessity of these traits can be recognized by anyone, even one who is not a qualified researcher and who does not in fact possess the traits in question. So where are we? We do not know that there is any truth in ethics because we have not searched for, much less found, any consensus among qualified researchers. We do not even know whether there are indeed any such qualified researchers, much less what their beliefs are. So where are we? Have we gained anything at all by following Socrates in his search? We have indeed gained a great deal, but in order to see this we need to consolidate what we have gained by contrasting where we are (now) from where we once were and where our culture is now. Having done so, we will be prepared for the next step.

GENERAL CONCLUSION

Looking Back, Looking Ahead

Traits of the qualified researcher in ethics:

(1) Purity of heart, a resolute willingness to search for the truth about the Big Picture no matter what the cost that truth imposes on oneself or others, supported by:

the belief that truth regarding the Big Picture *may* exist;
the belief that the possession of knowledge regarding the Big Picture *may* be of great value or that the search for it is something important in its own right;
the belief that the researcher himself *may* lack full knowledge of the truth regarding the Big Picture; and
the belief that truth regarding the Big Picture *may* be discovered and knowledge gained by the correct exercise of reason.

(2) Logical and dialectical skills:

an understanding of the logical patterns of sound argument;

a readiness to demand logical consistency for the positions held by any given participant in the dialogue, whether oneself or others;

the ability to ask the right questions and to ask them in the right order;

the ability to distinguish what is relevant to the truth/falsity of a position from what is not relevant; and

specific abilities in logic and dialectic, including the ability to:

recognize the direction of causal order;

recognize the "structure of ordered properties" in a thing;

be clear about the point at issue;

be clear about the meaning of the terms used in the discussion;

recognize the order in which a discussion should proceed;

use hypotheses effectively;

recognize the level of precision and certitude a particular topic permits; and

recognize what forms of refutation are "worthless so far as truth is concerned."

(3) The possession of relevant knowledge, expertise.

(4) Features pertaining to systematic order:

the ability to focus on order and causal connections without being distracted either by excessive attention to similarities and dissimilarities obvious to the senses or by the pleasures and pains of the nonrational parts of the soul;

a readiness to attend to the possibility of systematic

interconnections among the features of the cosmos and an ability to note those interconnections where they exist; and

an appreciation of the importance of the so-called Dionysian Principle, that "good results from a single and integral (whole) cause, evil from a single defect," and its many applications.

(5) Moderation in the "spirited" part of the soul:

courage, readiness to face danger or evil without shrinking back;

honesty, readiness to be open and candid about one's true beliefs;

patience, readiness to endure some evil with calmness and composure;

magnanimity, readiness to rise above petty resentment and disregard insults or displays of ill temper by others;

absence of arrogance, readiness to avoid any undue assumption with respect to one's knowledge, abilities, or importance;

docility, readiness to receive instruction from others;

gentleness, readiness to be mild and kind toward the person with whom one is engaged in dialectic;

good will, genuine concern for the well being of the person with whom one is engaged in dialectic, especially as the other person's well being relates to his knowing the truth;

charity, genuine concern to understand the other person's point of view and the reasons that could be offered for his position; and fairness, readiness to treat all positions and arguments in a similar and consistent manner.

(6) Moderation in the "appetitive" part of the soul, an effective readiness to subject the desires of the appetitive part of the soul to the rational part, so that the assessments by reason are not obscured or distorted by the desire for pleasure or possessions.

A Look Back

"And now the measure of our song is done, the work has reached its end, the book is ours." To see what is "ours," we need to pause and think about where we were before we began accompanying Socrates on his search for moral truth. Where, then, were we? Obviously, each of us began this search from (at least slightly) different starting points, but we can provide a general account by looking to the culture from which most of us have come—late postmodern western culture. We have examined our traits and defended them dialectically, so presumably we are now all together regarding them. And where remains western culture? As we shall see, at considerable distance from our present location. If we began from anywhere near where western culture resides now, we have completed a very long journey indeed. To demonstrate this point, let us take the traits we have uncovered while accompanying Socrates on his search for moral truth and see how sharply they differ from typical ways of thinking in our culture. Our reflections will reveal major differences in four areas.

A general observation before we begin. None of the differences we are going to highlight constitutes a sharp, night-and-day difference, the total presence versus the total absence of some feature. The differences are all matters of degree, but they are all none the less "true enough to be worth saying." We should keep this point in mind regarding each of the differences.

Difference One: The Sheer Difficulty of Adequate Moral Thought (Traits 2, 3, 4)

Adequate moral thought is extremely difficult. Not everyone is capable of providing much illumination regarding a particular moral topic. Not everyone (to put it mildly) possesses a signifcant number of the traits necessary for a qualified researcher in the field of ethics, and someone who is reasonably (even if imperfectly) qualified will easily and immediately recognize that this is so. But why is this so?

First, recall the dialectical traits under the second trait. Some of these are technical skills that can take years to acquire and develop. It may be easy to name and admit their importance, but these are habits of mind whose possession is no small accomplishment even for those researchers who set out with determination to acquire and master. In our culture one commonly hears that these are "difficult moral questions," but it impresses me as being far from the mind of those making such statements that these "difficult questions" can best be answered only by researchers possessing these traits.

Second, recall the complexities alluded to under the fourth trait. If there is a truth about the Big Picture, about the best life I can possibly live, then that truth may involve systematic interconnections among features related to one another in ways not obvious to the senses. Certainly, as we have seen, their non-existence should not be assumed at the outset; rather, we must be on the lookout for them, and our attention must be broader in scope than is generally recognized. I remember a person once saying, "I do not need someone else to tell me what to do." Later I thought to myself, "Well, that depends on what you want to do." If you want to perform brain surgery and you are not trained in that specialty, then perhaps you would be well advised after all to do what you are told. There is a common, deep assumption in our culture that living the best life is much, much less complicated than conducting brain surgery. Is it?

Third, recall the importance of relevant knowledge and expertise. When we introduced this trait in chapter 7, we briefly mentioned some of the many areas in which the qualified researcher needed to be informed. If there is a truth about the Big Picture, about the best way to conduct one's *whole life*, then that knowledge regarding the likely effects of various actions needs to be broad indeed. Now it is true that our culture tends to recognize the importance of knowledge and expertise, but it does so in a remarkable fashion—the more specialized the question, the more information needed; the broader the question, the less information needed. The discussion-stopping question—"who is to say?"—becomes more effective in proportion to the scope of the question raised. Again, if there is a truth about the Big Picture, the truth is likely to be much more complex and discovering it is likely to present a much greater challenge than our culture seems to suppose.

Difference Two: The Sheer Difficulty of Exercising Virtues of the Spirited Part (Trait 5)

Our culture recognizes the importance of the fifth trait, *but not in connection with topics related directly to the Big Picture*. It does praise many of these traits in different settings; some of these traits are valued simply as ways of being nice. You are not a nice person if you lack them. But that the exercise of these traits is vital for the discovery of moral truth, on this our culture is silent.

Patience: if discovering how to live the best possible life is a difficult matter, it will not be achieved in a few bull sessions, not even after a couple of semesters in high school, not even with half a dozen college courses under my belt. Courage: if the people with whom I am speaking fall significantly short of being qualified researchers in the field of ethics, then a readiness to discuss with them in spite of this lack takes some doing. This applies equally to honesty, magnanimity, gentleness, and good will. Fairness: if I have a natural desire to show myself in the right and others in the wrong, to justify myself and my way of living, then the fair and unbiased examination of each argument and position as it presents itself is going to be a major achievement. This applies equally to absence of arrogance, docility, and charity.

Difference Three: The Sheer Difficulty of Exercising Virtues of the Appetitive Part (Trait 6)

I believe the passages of most direct and immediate practical relevance in this entire book are those pertaining to moderation of the "many-headed beast" in chapter 11, and especially Plato's statement regarding the fact that "every pleasure or pain has something like a nail and nails the soul to the body and impedes it and makes it body-like, believing to be true whatever the body might say" (*Phaedo* 83d). In chapter 11, I referred to this condition as a "binding" and a "blinding," a self-binding and a self-blinding—a binding and subjugation of the rational part to the whims of the spirited and appetitive parts, a blinding of the rational part to whatever the bodily senses and pleasures and pains do not certify. We very much desire pleasures, possessions, and status. We very much want to acquire them without the rational part's objections. We find it quite easy to agree with Callicles—though we are likely to place restrictions on *his* unrestricted declaration—that "luxury and licentiousness and liberty, if held in abundance, this is excellence and happiness" (492c). As we saw in that chapter, the binding and blinding can occur not only when our own interests are involved but also when the interests of some specially favored individual or group is at issue, some person or group of persons for whom we have particular regard, fondness, or pity. Our culture is quick to detect (or imagine or project) this blinding in *others*, those, for instance, who are said to "cling" to one thing or another; that this is a pervasive, deeply-rooted feature of the human condition our culture is not so quick to admit. A forthright and serious admission of that feature could conceivably impose severe restrictions on the gratification of my desires.

Difference Four: A General Disregard for the Possible Existence of Moral Knowledge (Trait 1)

The prevalence of the remark (it typically is not really taken as a question) "who is to say?" is an indication of a general cultural disregard for the possible existence of moral truth, though members of our culture are not always fully consistent and critically self-aware in this regard. To illustrate: if someone were to say that child prostitution is terribly wrong and I were to respond with "who is to say?" I would be thought crazy or otherwise seriously ill. But if I were to push the dialectical endeavor beyond polite limits and the other person were willing to engage, I believe few (at least of those unmotivated by religious doctrine) would finally respond, "Well, it *is* wrong and I just *know* it is." Long before we reached that point I would have shown him that other societies have not always taken such an absolute view of the matter, and I would have asked him who he thought he was, imposing his *own personal* views on someone else. I am pretty confident that in this way I could wear down the vast majority of the (nonreligious) members of our culture, forcing them back into the last defense—"we just do not allow that here." Not all, but the vast majority. Few would be sufficiently bold to continue maintaining that the practice simply is wrong and they know it to be so.

We have seen that the argument from unresolved widespread disagreement plays an important role in this regard. Not only does the argument seem to work, but as we noted in the opening "Apology," the argument has a not insignificant payoff. If there is no moral truth then there are no limits to what a person's Big Picture may contain, short of not getting caught or doing something that bothers his emotional life, and Callicles's "luxury and licentiousness and liberty, if held in abundance," really are "excellence and happiness." I do not pretend to know how important a role this last consideration plays in the mind of the typical member of our culture, but it remains available for those who desire to use it.

A second possible support for (and perhaps consequence of) the argument from unresolved widespread disagreement is our culture's equally widespread misology regarding topics related to the Big Picture. That misology, as we saw at the end of chapter 7, often results from an ignorance of the traits discussed in that chapter, the features under trait (2). Any individual or culture not conversant with the many skills there discussed (see Difference One) is going to be at significant risk for suffering the harm of misology.

The Moon Is a Harsh Mistress is the title of a book I have never read and probably never will, but its title captures my interest. When I recall it, though, I usually substitute "Reality" for "The Moon"—reality is a harsh mistress. If reality is indeed a harsh mistress, it will be unforgiving when ignored or held in disdain, but as we have seen, forcing oneself to attend to that reality is not without its own costs.

With this in mind, take a good hard look at the face of the young man on the book cover, the young man whom Socrates, notorious for his ugliness, so earnestly addresses. He is Alcibiades (451–404 B.C.), he of the "does this man *ever* stop talking?" expression. This identification with Alcibiades is a minority view, but who else could Raphael have had in mind to produce such a striking portrait? The history of Alcibiades's life and death suffices to show the importance of paying attention to reality. Alcibiades was descended from families on both his father's and his mother's side who were among the most wealthy and influential in Athens. After his father died he became a ward of Pericles, the single most powerful man in Athens. Alcibiades was an excellent leader in battle and renowned as a persuasive speaker, and he used his wealth to further his power. Several of Plato's dialogues portray Alcibiades's association with Socrates, an association which ultimately benefitted neither party. In 415, during the Peloponnesian War (431–404), Alcibiades persuaded the Athenian assembly to attack Sicily, a debacle from which Athens never recovered, and he served as one of the generals of the doomed expedition. Charged with having profaned the Eleusinian mysteries and being summoned to return to Athens and stand trial, Alcibiades defected to the enemy Sparta, but then in 411 was prevailed upon to side again with the Athenian forces and was given command of an Athenian fleet, and then later named "general-in-chief with absolute authority." A naval defeat in 407 led to his being dismissed from command and he retired from the war, though in 406 many in Athens were still calling for his return. The accounts of his assassination in 404 differ, though most involve the Spartans in some fashion, perhaps still fearful of the power he held over the Athenian assembly.[1] Alcibiades—wealthy, powerful, charming, persuasive, murdered at 47 years of age—is a warning to us of how harsh a mistress reality can be.

1. Debra Nails, *The People of Plato: A Prosopography of Plato and Other Socratics* (Indianapolis, Ind.: Hackett, 2002), 11–16.

Conclusion

Comfort for Echecrates: An Argument for the Existence of Moral Knowledge

We have conducted this book's search in a manner independent of any assumption that moral truth and moral knowledge do in fact exist. In preparation for the task that remains to us after the close of this book, we need to present an actual argument for their existence. Genuine moral truth does exist and we do possess genuine moral knowledge. And if we are assured that there does exist *some* moral truth and that we do possess *some* moral knowledge, then the spell by which we have been blinded and bound is dispelled, and we are prepared for the next step: if there is *some* moral knowledge available to us, how can there be just this *some*?

The argument I am about to present I attempted to make more than twenty years ago in two companion articles which, in the lovely words of David Hume (1711–76), together "fell dead-born from the press, without reaching such distinction as even to excite a murmur among the zealots."[2] But there may be some life in them yet, so let me try to resuscitate these two articles. The overall argument falls into three parts: a preliminary softening up and then two direct arguments.

Plato provides us with a nice opening cannonade: "Does it profit anyone who in order to acquire gold unjustly enslaves the best part of himself to the most depraved? If in acquiring gold he sold his son or daughter into slavery to savage and evil men, it would not profit him, no matter how much gold he acquired by doing so" (*Re-*

2. David Hume, "My Own Life," in *An Enquiry Concerning Human Understanding and Other Writings*, ed. Stephen Buckle (Cambridge: Cambridge University Press, 2007), 216. The two articles are "Moral Knowledge and 'The Argument from Queerness,'" *American Catholic Philosophical Quarterly* 44, no. 2 (Spring 1990): 215–32; "On the View that Nothing Matters," *Journal of Value Inquiry* 26, no. 2 (April 1992): 251–59.

public 589de). Let us take up Plato's suggestion and develop a tale in which two parents sell their son and daughter to a trans-national organization trading in child prostitution. The parents had seen a television news report on the organization which showed the condition of the child prostitutes to be horrible. Most viewers found the report almost unbearable to watch, but the program gave the parents a very good idea indeed, and they followed up the leads in the program, made contact with the organization, and completed a deal to sell their children, and because both children were so beautiful, the parents demanded and got top dollar. Their only regret was that they had no more children left to sell. The parents were not in any financial straits, the money was in no way necessary for them, but they planned to make a few purchases they had been eyeing. They had high confidence in a scheme to explain their children's disappearance. Watching the show had turned out to be a fortunate occurrence.

Was the behavior of the parents wrong? You (a typical representative of our culture) do not like it, of course, but the parents do. Society disapproves and the parents would go to jail and be the objects of universal loathing were they found out, but so what? You might be inclined to say that this behavior was wrong, but do you *know* that it was wrong, or only that you intensely dislike it? On the other hand, the parents intensely like it, and *who is to say* whether you or they are correct? There may be, in fact, widespread agreement about the wrongfulness of the parents' behavior; only the parents think it right. But was there not supposed to be *no* truth about ethics, the Big Picture, *at all, no* knowledge to be had *at all*? Is there or is there not? Is it not really the case that you have just lost your (clarity of) mind here, that your emotional dislike of the act has momentarily overcome your recognition of the *real truth*, that there just *is no genuine truth* to be had about the Big Picture? Do not get carried away by your emotions; remain calm; keep repeating to yourself this truth: "Although I intensely dislike and most everybody else intensely dislikes the action of the parents, I must not confuse intense dislike with any objective wrongfulness of the act that can be known." You of course are free to do all in your power to see to it that such acts are prevented or punished simply because you (and your society) so intensely dislike them, but you may (must) not confuse that with any belief that the action in question really is wrong, that your emotional reaction possesses any reasoned basis, any rational justification.

In the second of my two articles I used (borrowed) the expression of a person's being "de-souled," of missing a piece of his soul. The view expressed in the previous paragraph is the view of a person de-souled, missing part of his soul. He is missing (the use of) his reason. His emotional parts are there, but his rational part is not. If his rational part were in place and employed correctly, he would have been able to recognize the *truth* that the parents' action is *inconsistent* with living a good and successful and flourishing human life, that the parents' action *must* contribute to a failed, miserable, and wretched life. In Plato's words, "Does it *ever* profit anyone who in order to acquire gold unjustly enslaves the best part of himself ["the man"] to the most depraved ["the many-headed beast"]?"

The person is de-souled who fails to use one of the parts of his soul in accordance with its proper function. Our rational power was given to us (whether by God or evolution) to *use*, and one of the uses of our reason is to employ *it* (and not our emotional parts) to figure out how best to live. The person who does not use his reason to figure out which of the many competing Big Pictures are genuinely worthwhile is a person who has brought only a *part* of his soul to his life. He is de-souled.

How is this de-soulment brought about? Physical causes such

as blows to the head or tumors in the brain can produce many different forms of de-soulment, but the ones of interest to us are the *moral* causes mentioned in chapter 11: enchantment, force, and theft. The first two moral causes are self-administered, the third may be introduced by the self or by someone else. The three causes are most effective when they all work together supporting one another. Children naturally believe that some things really are right/good and that other things really are wrong/bad. In order to believe differently, they have to be carefully taught something quite different, either by themselves or by others.

As we grow in age and "mature," we discover that many actions we were taught to be wrong turn out to be pleasant, whereas many actions we were taught to be right turn out to be painful. What to do? Three options present themselves: (1) we can continue to hold those old beliefs; (2) we can change our beliefs about them, holding now that the pleasant actions are in fact good after all, the painful actions in fact bad (these first two options may or may not be motivated by purely rational considerations); or (3) we can adopt the view that there is not really anything that is truly good or truly bad but that it is up to each person to decide for himself whether he is going to treat the thing as good for him or bad for him. Of course, it may be that the beliefs we acquired in childhood were in fact mistaken, but if they were true, then adopting the second or third options can be eased by application of enchantment and force. The third option can also be fostered by the argument from unresolved widespread disagreement, which this book has shown to be a very poor argument indeed, an instance of Socratic "theft."

We are now suitably prepared for the first direct argument. When we recognize that some action is good, another bad, we are recognizing, even if only in the faintest of ways, how the action stands with respect to the order constituting human excellence and flourishing and ultimately with respect to the order of the cosmos. Order is a feature of reality that cannot be grasped by the senses but only by reason; if we are de-souled in the manner mentioned above, order is a feature of reality to which we must be blind. As it is, we do not pay much explicit attention to the cosmos when we think and act, but it nonetheless forms the unobtrusive background against which all our straightforward moral thinking (unaffected by enchantment, force, or theft) takes place. Let us consider some examples.

A considerable number of words in the English language refer to traits of persons which everyone "instinctively" recognizes to be either required for living the best life one can possibly live or incompatible with it. Consider two lists, A and B:

> A: benevolent, candid, charitable, circumspect, civil, compassionate, conscientious, considerate, cordial, courteous, diligent, discerning, disciplined, discrete, flexible, generous, gentle, honest, hospitable, kind, magnanimous, patient, provident, reliable, resilient, resolute, resourceful, responsive, sensible, sensitive, spirited, tender, thoughtful, warm.

> B: anorexic, apathetic, arbitrary, arrogant, avaricious, bigoted, bitter, bloodthirsty, brutal, bulimic, bully, captious, careless, censorious, conceited, contentious, cranky, crass, craven, credulous, cruel, cynical, envious, erratic, feckless, flighty, fretful, frivolous, grandiose, grasping, groveling, heedless, improvident, inconstant, incurious, indolent, irresponsible, irritable, malicious, mean, mercenary, merciless, mercurial, misanthropic, miserly, misogynic, morbid, morose, nagging, narcissistic, opinionated, paranoid, peevish, petulant, pretentious, puerile, pusillanimous, querulous, rancorous, rapacious, rash, resentful, rude, sanctimonious, savage, servile, shallow, shameless, short-tempered, silly, small-minded, smug, snide, splenetic, stiff-necked, stingy, superficial, superstitious, surly, suspicious, sycophantic, temperamental, thoughtless, truculent, unctuous, ungrateful, unreasonable, virulent, vindictive, venal, wasteful, willful.

Each of these words means something. Each refers to a trait someone might possess. The meaning of any of these words can be checked by looking up the word in a good dictionary. The idea here is that anyone who is clear about the meaning of a given word will immediately be able to see that the trait is part of the best life one can live (if the trait is from list A) or is excluded by such a life (if the trait is from list B). The basis for the ability to sort these traits into these two categories is the power which is natural to us as rational animals, our rational power, the ability to recognize order in contrast to disorder. By way of illustration, let us take a pair of examples, one from each list. The same process can be used with any of the words to support the same point: *we do possess moral knowledge*. Let us take "reliable" and "cruel." You can establish the point for yourself by selecting your own pair, and you are earnestly encouraged to do so.

What is important is not the actual word selected ("reliable") but the *trait* the word picks out, namely, "that may be relied upon; in which reliance may be put; trustworthy, safe, sure." Now of course, the trait of reliability may be put to bad use: trustworthy conspirators who can be counted upon to perform their roles in some embezzlement scheme, for instance. But this is the question: is the trait of being a reliable person an important and necessary part of leading the best life possible? I think the answer is clearly yes, and anyone who is engaged in "straightforward moral thinking" can see that the answer is clearly yes. We are rational beings and the power of rationality is the power to recognize order. The Big Picture possesses a structure, an order, and reliability is recognized by our rational power as indissolubly connected with it. Put it this way: can we not clearly and indisputably recognize that a person simply *cannot* lead the best life possible without possessing reliability in any degree regarding anything? Anyone who wishes to argue dialectically to the contrary is of course encouraged to do so.

Now for "cruel," defined as "disposed to inflict suffering; indifferent to or taking pleasure in another's pain or distress; destitute of kindness or compassion; merciless, pitiless, hard-hearted." Here the rational animal sees manifest disorder, the life associated with a brigand. Again, everyone is free to argue the contrary. See what you can come up with for "cruel." Do you find your counter-arguments compelling, plausible, laughable? Remember that in assessing your arguments you must call into play the full range of dialectical virtues.

I developed those two lists more than twenty years ago in order to make this general point: we do possess moral knowledge, and this knowledge is grounded on our rational ability to distinguish order from disorder. We tend to assign misplaced importance to the argument from unresolved widespread disagreement at least in part because our culture has *taught* us to assign the argument such importance. What we have *not* been taught by our culture is the importance of being a qualified researcher in the field of ethics. Also, our culture assigns a very high importance to being tolerant and nonjudgmental. There are no doubt many respectable reasons for being tolerant and nonjudgmental, but there are limits. Tolerance and nonjudgmentalism can be carried too far, and when they are carried too far they can be summoned to provide remarkably effective supports for allowing a person to do pretty much whatever he feels like doing at the time. They are also highly effective in bringing about the de-soulment of both individual and culture.

Now the second direct argument. Thomas Hobbes (1588–1679) was an English philosopher whose ideas frightened people. He was born in the year the "invincible" Spanish Armada threatened England (unsuccessfully, it turned out, much to the surprise of nearly everyone on both sides), writing "And here upon it was my mother dear / Did bring forth twins at once, both me, and fear" of the Armada.[3] Hobbes himself was afraid of chaos and anarchy, but

3. "Vita carmine expressa," in *Thomas Hobbes Malmesburiensis Opera Philosophica Quae Latina Scripsit Omnia*, ed. William Molesworth (London: John Bohm, 1839): 1:86.

many of his contemporaries were afraid of Hobbes, that is, of the ideas Hobbes espoused. Hobbes argued that what we think of as common morality is simply the content of an agreement we adopt with one another to protect ourselves from the conditions of a state of nature in which the stronger prey ruthlessly on the weaker, a condition, it turns out, eerily like the one strongly advocated by Callicles. Prior to this social contract, there simply is no morality as we commonly think of it. Prior to the social contract and in the state of nature, "morality" allows us to do absolutely whatever we believe will in some way promote our survival. In such a condition the life of man is "solitary, poor, nasty, brutish, and short."[4]

This idea of a natural "war of all against all" was frightening to contemplate for Hobbes's contemporaries, and many devoted significant effort to refute him. One of his most able critics was Samuel Clarke (1675–1729). Clarke maintained that there are many moral assertions which are both (1) true *prior* to any "social contract" among human beings and (2) *known* to be true by anyone who has the least bit of understanding. Clarke writes:

> In Men's dealing and conversing with one another, 'tis undeniably more Fit, absolutely and in the nature of the thing itself, that All Men should endeavor to promote the universal good and welfare of All, than that all Men should be continually contriving the ruin and destruction of All. 'Tis evidently more Fit, even before all positive Bargains and Compacts [Clarke clearly has Hobbes in mind here], that Men should deal one with another according to the known Rules of Justice and Equity, than that every Man for his own present Advantage, should without scruple disappoint the most reasonable and equitable Expectations of his Neighbors, and cheat and defraud, or spoil by violence, all others without restraint. Lastly, 'tis without dispute more Fit and reasonable in itself, that I should preserve the life of an innocent Man, that happens to be at any time in my Power,

4. *Leviathan*, in *The English Works of Thomas Hobbes*, ed. William Molesworth (London: John Bohm, 1839), 3:113.

or to deliver him from any imminent danger, 'tho I have never made any promise so to do [Hobbes again], than that I should suffer him to perish, or take away his life, without any reason or provocation at all.[5]

"Fit" here can be taken to mean "fitting into the order of things." Clarke maintains that with regard to moral truths like these, "nothing but the extremist stupidity of Mind, corruption of Manners, or perverseness of Spirit can possibly make any Man entertain the least doubt concerning them" (484). Denying knowledge of them is tantamount to denying the existence of order in the world. Again, are you able to provide arguments for denying the truth of Clarke's statements? What would you say of those arguments if you possessed purity of heart?

With other topics the truth is not so obvious because *either* the order/disorder is not so manifest *or* our not being qualified researchers poses a real obstacle to seeing the truth, or both. Other topics may be much more complex than the ones mentioned here, or they may present themselves in such a way as to provide targets of opportunity for enchantment, force, and their ally theft. Where do we go from here?

A Look Ahead: A Statue of Daedalus for the Present Age?

We begin our next step from our current cultural situation. I have no magic wand to wave; if I did, my "rewards would be many and great," but what I do have to offer may be of some help. Keep in mind the following observation: *Qualified researchers in the field of ethics are rare.* Two corollaries immediately follow: *I am not likely to be a qualified researcher in the field of ethics*, and *the person with whom I am speaking is not likely to be a qualified researcher in the field of ethics*. There

5. *A Discourse Concerning the Unchangeable Obligations of Natural Religion*, excerpted in *The British Moralists*, ed. L. A. Selby-Bigge (New York: Bobbs-Merrill, 1964), 2:5–6.

are three reasons for this. First, becoming a qualified researcher is extremely difficult even for someone who both understands what it is to be one and genuinely desires to become one. Second, most people do not understand what a qualified researcher in the field of ethics is, and it is difficult (if not impossible) to become one without that understanding. Third, most people lack a sufficient desire to become a qualified researcher in the field of ethics, and it is nearly (if not completely) impossible to become one without that desire.

Being a qualified researcher in the field of ethics is a matter of degree and subject to growth and decay. Even when I take this observation seriously, I should not become discouraged either with myself or others. As we saw in chapter 11, patience in these matters is an essential virtue. I can acknowledge my own shortcomings and not be surprised when I encounter those of others, and still pursue the discussion as far as it can profitably be taken. And if "practice" does not make "perfect," practice can at least make for improvement.

It is a good strategy to adopt the role of questioner. Immediately after Socrates had demolished Gorgias with his questioning, he asked Polus whether he preferred to continue the discussion by doing the questioning or the answering; to this Polus unsurprisingly responded that *he* would do the asking (462b). As it turned out, Polus was unable to maintain that role very long and was flattened as Gorgias had been. Still, Polus was on to something; it is much easier to ask questions than to answer them, and knowing what questions to ask and when to ask them is a matter of learning through practice. So find out what the other person knows; maybe he knows a lot, even if you do not agree with him on the issue under discussion. In doing so you can also discover whether the other person is like Socrates and Gorgias who are searching for the truth or is one who simply wants to win.

It is perfectly appropriate to quit a discussion. If the other person seems to possess little pertinent knowledge or to lack much of a desire to discover the truth about the topic, then simply change the subject.

You are under no obligation to "win" a discussion. If you push your questioning far and skillfully, the other person is likely to ask you what you think and probe for your reasons. See this as an opportunity! Believe me, there is nothing in the rules that says you must "win" here. Rather, you have a chance of finding out what you know and what you do not know, and this is good. You say exactly what you think, along with your reasoning, and then let the other person have his say. Either he has a response or he does not; if he does, his responses/objections may be silly or they may have merit (and always be careful in accepting the former possibility) or they may be mixtures of both. If they are silly, you may suggest why they are; if they have merit, you will need to do some thinking about them, either then or later. The person may listen to you and be willing to work with you, or he may not. If the former, keep going; if the latter, quit.

You should try to continue a discussion for as long as it is profitable. Precisely because a good discussion is so valuable in the pursuit of truth, it should not be terminated prematurely. One highly useful way of doing this is to divide the points of disagreement into as many as possible, and then examine each one separately and pursue each as far as possible. For instance, suppose I am holding that A did something bad because he did B, and the other person disagrees. Here is how one can divide the points of possible disagreement into as many as possible. Did A in fact do B? Is it bad to do B no matter who does it? Is doing B identical to doing X-Y-Z? The first deals with fact, the second with principle, and the third with definition. It is rather unlikely that the other person and I disagree on all these points. Find as many points of agreement as possible, reducing still-disputed issues to a minimum. Agreeing on whatever can be agreed upon is an excellent means of building trust and good will toward one another.

It is perfectly acceptable to defer a discussion to a later time. If the person seems to possess a desire to pursue the truth and has interesting things to say, then the following remark is quite appropriate: "You have made some very good points and I do not feel satisfied with the answers I might give you, so let me think about them further and we can speak about them at some future time." Maybe the other person is correct and you are mistaken; if so, you should be grateful to the person and thank him. Or, maybe you are not sure and need to do more thinking or ask others for help. Dialectic is a common endeavor for the pursuit of truth, and to be engaged in a good discussion, especially when interrupted as it can be, really is a fortunate occurrence and should be recognized as such.

You should always be on the lookout for systematic and long-term features pertinent to the issue. In the conclusion to part 2 we defended the importance of attention to systematic interconnections. To be informed of these traits and admit their importance is unfortunately a far cry from being adept in them. This sad fact is true for almost all the traits of the qualified researcher in the field of ethics. It is one thing to understand their importance and to genuinely desire to possess them; it is quite another to actually possess them, even if only in a rudimentary degree. Patience! Simply attending to their importance and genuinely desiring to possess them is the beginning.

You should always attend to the Dionysian Principle. Some policy, program, or action may look good, but there is always more to the story. Now perhaps the rest of the story is not all that important in a given case, but do not ever suppose this is so before doing one's best to find out. The unwarranted inference from "this feature of P is good" to the conclusion "P is itself good" may be the most common mistake in moral reasoning. In addition, *you should be hesitant to declare an issue settled.* This is not to say that nothing is ever settled, but it is obvious that one needs to be careful. Traits (2), (3), and (4) highlight how careful one should be.

You should trust reason as something most valuable, but recognize and submit to its limits. Traits (2) and (3) are particularly relevant here, especially concerning statistical argumentation. Everyone knows the expression "lies, damn lies, and statistics," and no wonder. The function of reason is the discovery of truth, and statistical analysis is a powerful tool, but it can be misleading.

You should practice as sincerely as you can traits pertaining to the "spirited" part of the soul. The traits of honesty, magnanimity, absence of arrogance, docility, good will, charity, fairness are not easy ones to acquire. Beginning with "I have an opinion on P but it is very possible that I am wrong, so I would like to hear your thoughts on it" is a good start. Find out what the other person has to say, pushing for his reasons, and then be willing if asked to say what you think and provide your reasons. It may go well, it may not. But you can learn from failure, and failure is an excellent means of acquiring these traits. Gilbert Keith Chesterton (1874–1936) wrote, "If a thing is worth doing, it is worth doing badly."[6] Nowhere is this truer than for becoming a qualified researcher in the field of ethics. The corollary: *You should always be sensitive to how the other person stands with regard to traits of the "spirited" part.* If the other person seems to possess some of the traits, it may be a good idea to commend him for it. If he seems to lack them, you might think about pointing this out to him, but doing so may end the discussion immediately, so be careful. On the other hand, a discussion with someone seriously

6. *What's Wrong with the World* (London: Cassell, 1916), 254.

lacking many of these traits is unlikely to be productive in the discovery of truth.

You should practice as sincerely as you can traits pertaining to the "appetitive" part of the soul. The previous point pertains as much to my relationship with the other person as it does to myself alone, whereas this point pertains more to myself. It may generally be the case that the single biggest obstacle to my discovering the truth is *my own* failure to subordinate the "appetitive" part of my soul to the rational. The corollary: *You should always be sensitive to how the other person stands with regard to traits of the "appetitive" part.*

Purity of heart is a matter of degree and subject to growth and to decay. And the corollary: *practice as sincerely as you can purity of heart.* Purity of heart, the resolute willingness to search for the truth about the Big Picture no matter what the cost that truth imposes on oneself or others, is the key to success in becoming a qualified researcher in the field of ethics. Without purity of heart, success is flatly impossible. With purity of heart, the rest will take care of itself. I may lack natural intellectual ability. I may get easily flustered. I may be forgetful or prone to frustration with myself or others. With purity of heart, even accompanied by my shortcomings, I will have reasoned as best I can.

Truly setting one's will is not an easy task; it is not a matter of reciting a formula even sincerely, but rather a matter of adopting a way of life. Socrates pointed out the way to us: "On the other points of the argument I would not stubbornly hold fast, but on this I do: believing we must search for what we do not know, we will be better and more courageous and less good-for-nothings than if we believe that what we do not know can be neither discovered nor searched for" (*Meno* 86bc). I am not the kind of person to say I would prefer to spend my life searching for knowledge rather than finding it. But I do side with Socrates here: we will be better and more courageous and less good-for-nothing human beings if we spend our lives searching for the knowledge we do not possess, even if we do not discover it, than if we do not search at all. Being a fully qualified researcher in the field of ethics is an ideal. Socrates discusses a topic very similar to this near the end of the *Republic*, a dialogue which (among many other things) examines the nature of the ideal human community (592ab):

> G: [The wise person] will not wish to engage in political affairs....
>
> S: Yes, by the dog, in his *own* city [the ideal one] and very much so, yet perhaps not in his native city....
>
> G: Now I understand. You mean in the city we were constructing as we spoke, in the city existing in the realm of reason, for I think it to be nowhere on the earth.
>
> S: Well, perhaps in heaven a paradigm is set up [like a trophy or votive offering] *for the one wishing to behold it and so beholding to dwell therein.*

There surely is a pattern of the qualified researcher in ethics, one set up in heaven for the wise person to behold and so beholding to dwell therein. Can you feel the pattern taking on life?

BIBLIOGRAPHY

Aristotle. *Aristotelis Ethica Nicomachea.* Edited by J. Bywater. Oxford: Oxford University Press, 1894.

———. *Aristotelis Topica et Sophistici Elenchi.* Edited by W. D. Ross. Oxford: Oxford University Press, 1958.

Atkinson, Gary. "Moral Knowledge and 'The Argument from Queerness.'" *American Catholic Philosophical Quarterly* 44, no. 2 (Spring 1990): 215–32.

———. "On the View that Nothing Matters." *Journal of Value Inquiry* 26, no. 2 (April 1992): 251–59.

Carroll, Lewis. *Alice's Adventures in Wonderland and Through the Looking Glass.* Oxford: Oxford University Press, 1998.

Chesterton, G. K. *What's Wrong with the World.* London: Cassell, 1916.

Clarke, Samuel. *A Discourse Concerning the Unchangeable Obligations of Natural Religion*, excerpted in *The British Moralists.* Edited by L. A. Selby-Bigge. New York: Bobbs-Merrill, 1964.

Compact Edition of the Oxford English Dictionary. Oxford: Oxford University Press, 1971.

Hobbes, Thomas. *Leviathan*, in *The English Works of Thomas Hobbes.* Edited by William Molesworth (London: John Bohm, 1839), 3:113.

———. "Vita carmine expressa," in *Thomas Hobbes Malmesburiensis Opera Philosophica Quae Latina Scripsit Omnia*. Edited by William Molesworth. London: John Bohm, 1839.

Hume, David. "My Own Life," in *An Enquiry Concerning Human Understanding and Other Writings*. Edited by Stephen Buckle. Cambridge: Cambridge University Press, 2007.

Nails, Debra. *The People of Plato: A Prosopography of Plato and Other Socratics.* Indianapolis, Ind.: Hackett, 2002.

Plato. *Platonis Opera.* 5 vols. Edited by John Burnet et al. Oxford: Oxford University Press, 1901–2011.

INDEX

Index

Our Search with Socrates for Moral Truth was designed in Vendetta Light with Perpetua Titling and Arno display type and composed by Kachergis Book Design of Pittsboro, North Carolina. It was printed on 60-pound Natures Recycled and bound by McNaughton & Gunn of Saline, Michigan.